SpeedPro Series

HOW TO BUILD & POWER TUNE
DISTRIBUTOR-TYPE
IGNITION SYSTEMS

NEW THIRD EDITION!

Des Hammill

Covers all traditional ignition systems that include a distributor • Applies to all
engine types • Tells you how to set up and modify the whole ignition system to get
optimum power from YOUR engine • Tells you how to time a modified engine
• Does not cover ECU-controlled distributorless systems

This book is dedicated to one of life's characters, my friend John Moran, who had the gift of telling really good jokes all day, he could literally reel them off one after the other. We were in stitches half of the day and it's a wonder that any work was done. Sadly, John died in December 1996 and life hasn't been the same on the joke front since.

First published in 1997. Reprinted 2000, 2002, 2003 & 2004. A full colour edition was published in 2005. This new third edition first published April 2009. Reprinted August 2017 by Veloce Publishing Limited, Veloce House, Parkway Farm Business Park, Poundbury, Dorchester, Dorset, D11 3AR, England. Fax 01305 250479/e-mail info@veloce.co.uk/web www.veloce.co.uk or www.velocebooks.com
ISBN 978-1-787111-73-8/UPC 6-36847-01173-4

SpeedPro Series

HOW TO BUILD & POWER TUNE
DISTRIBUTOR-TYPE
IGNITION SYSTEMS

NEW
THIRD
EDITION!

VELOCE PUBLISHING
THE PUBLISHER OF FINE AUTOMOTIVE BOOKS

Veloce *SpeedPro* books –

978-1-903706-59-6

978-1-903706-75-6

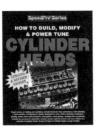
978-1-903706-76-3

978-1-903706-99-2

978-1-845840-21-1

978-1-787111-68-4

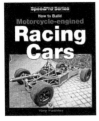
978-1-787111-69-1

978-1-787111-73-8

978-1-845841-87-4

978-1-845842-07-9

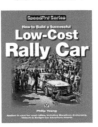
978-1-845842-08-6

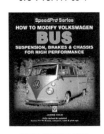
978-1-845842-62-8

978-1-845842-89-5

978-1-845842-97-0

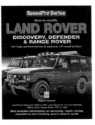
978-1-845843-15-1

978-1-845843-55-7

978-1-845844-33-2

978-1-845844-38-7

978-1-845844-83-7

978-1-845846-15-2

978-1-845848-33-0

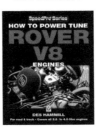
978-1-787111-76-9

978-1-845848-69-9

978-1-845849-60-3

978-1-845840-19-8

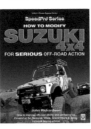
978-1-787110-92-2

978-1-787110-47-2

978-1-903706-94-7

978-1-787110-87-8

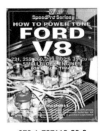
978-1-787110-90-8

978-1-787110-01-4

978-1-901295-26-9

978-1-845841-62-1

978-1-787110-91-5

978-1-787110-88-5

978-1-903706-78-7

Contents

Essential information & using this book

ESSENTIAL INFORMATION

This book contains information on practical procedures; however, this information is intended only for those with the qualifications, experience, tools and facilities to carry out the work in safety and with appropriately high levels of skill. Whenever working on a car or component, remember that your personal safety must **always** be your first consideration. The publisher, author, editors and retailer of this book cannot accept any responsibility for personal injury or mechanical damage which results from using this book, even if caused by errors or omissions in the information given. If this disclaimer is unacceptable to you, please return the pristine book to your retailer who will refund the purchase price.

In the text of this book **Warning** means that a procedure could cause personal injury and **Caution** that there is danger of mechanical damage if appropriate care is not taken. However,

be aware that we cannot possibly foresee every possibility of danger in every circumstance.

With regard to ignition systems there are two areas in particular which could cause personal injury. 1) Ignition system high tension wires carry very high voltages so always make sure your hands and your tools are appropriately insulated when working on a live ignition system. Don't work on live ignition systems if you are fitted with a pacemaker. 2) When using a stroboscope to illuminate timing marks on a running engine, tie back long hair and make sure that you are wearing no loose items of clothing/jewellery which could entangle in the engine's rotating/moving external components: keep the instrument's wires well clear of these components too. Keep your hands, arms and face well away from rotating/moving components.

Please note that changing component specification by modification is likely to void warranties and also

to absolve manufacturers from any responsibility in the event of component failure and the consequences of such failure.

Increasing the engine's power will place additional stress on engine components and on the car's complete driveline: this may reduce service life and increase the frequency of breakdown. An increase in engine power, and therefore the vehicle's performance, will mean that your vehicle's braking and suspension systems will need to be kept in perfect condition and uprated as appropriate.

The importance of cleaning a component thoroughly before working on it cannot be overstressed. Always keep your working area and tools as clean as possible. Whatever specialist cleaning fluid or other chemicals you use, be sure to follow – completely – manufacturer's instructions and, if you're using petrol (gasoline) or paraffin (kerosene) to clean parts, take every precaution necessary to protect your body and to avoid all risk of fire.

USING THIS BOOK

Throughout this book the text assumes that you, or your contractor, will have a workshop manual specific to your engine and ignition system components to follow for complete detail on dismantling, reassembly, adjustment procedure, clearances, torque figures, etc. This book's default is the standard manufacturer's specification/settings so, if a procedure is not described, a measurement not given, a torque figure ignored, you can assume that the standard manufacturer's procedure or specification for your equipment needs to be used.

You'll find it helpful to read the whole book before you start work or give instructions to your contractor. This is because a modification or change in specification in one area might cause the need for changes in other areas. Get the whole picture so that you can finalize specification and component requirements as far as is possible before any work begins.

Introduction

This book deals with distributor-type ignition systems. The distributor(s) can be of the contact breaker ('points') or electronic type – 'electronic' in this context meaning that some device other than points is used to make and break (switch on and off) the ignition low tension circuit.

Coverage of the ignition system within this book includes sparkplugs, plug wires (HT leads), ignition switches, coils, ignition modules, breaker points, twin point systems, caps, rotors, vacuum advance, and the mechanical advance mechanism in the distributor body.

This book also deals with reasons why various engine designs require a certain amount of ignition timing to produce maximum torque through to the point of maximum power, and how to arrive at, by test, what the correct amount of total ignition timing is for ANY engine, irrespective of its state of tune, or the fact that the amount of static and idle ignition timing required varies from engine to engine, as does the rate of

mechanical ignition timing advance.

Identifying the optimum amounts of static ignition timing, idle speed ignition timing, total ignition timing, and the optimum rate of ignition timing advance from idle to the total ignition timing point, are, perhaps, the most crucial issues for enthusiasts. These are also the features of ignition and ignition systems that people find the most baffling.

Note that static ignition timing is the amount present when the engine is not running – the idle ignition timing may or may not be the same. If an engine idles at 600-1000rpm or thereabouts, the static and idle amounts of ignition timing will almost always be the same, because there will usually be sufficient collective tension between the two mechanical advance springs, or in one of the advance springs, to prevent mechanical advance from increasing the static setting at such low engine rpm. However, road engines and racing engines often idle at 1000-1500rpm, at which point the speed of the centrifugal

weights in the advance mechanism might well have started to overcome the spring tension and now be advancing the ignition timing: such engines will then have different amounts of static and idle speed ignition timing. There's nothing wrong with this and in many instances it's actually very desirable, such as when the high amount of static ignition timing required is too much for the starter to turn the engine over quickly and surely.

This aspect of an ignition system is all to do with the amount of idle speed ignition timing required versus the rate of advance to the amount of total ignition timing required to produce maximum torque. If an engine requires 35 crankshaft degrees of total ignition timing to develop maximum torque between 3500-4500rpm, that amount of ignition timing is usually required to be 'all in' or fully advanced at about 3300rpm. If the engine idles smoothly at, say, 1100-1200rpm with 15 crankshaft degrees of idle speed ignition timing, the ignition timing requirements for optimum engine performance mean that the distributor is required to advance the ignition timing 10 distributor degrees or 20 crankshaft degrees between 1300rpm and 3300rpm, and springs of a particular tension will be required to do this. This is a simple example and, in such a case, the static ignition timing and the idle speed ignition timing will usually be 15 crankshaft degrees, because the mechanical advance mechanism springs won't allow the ignition timing to start advancing until 1300rpm is reached. The starter motor will need to be able to turn over and start the engine with this amount of static ignition timing (usually at 60-90rpm cranking speed). To start an engine, the minimum starter motor rpm required will be in the region of 60rpm. However, some of the very powerful, geared starters available these days can turn engines over at about 120rpm, or even more.

This book includes instructions and details on how to modify a distributor's total mechanical advance to suit **any** engine's state of tune, irrespective of what the performance modifications are.

Many engines are modified for high-performance use with little thought given to the ignition system. Vast amounts of time and money are spent on modifying an engine after which the original distributor is refitted and timed at the original factory recommended settings, with no thought being given to the amount of advance the modified engine is likely to need. That's the amount of static ignition timing for starting purposes, the idle speed ignition timing requirement, amount of total ignition timing required, the rate of the ignition timing advance from the idle speed to the 'all in' total amount. If this vital aspect of engine tuning is ignored, it is exceedingly unlikely that the particular engine concerned will ever produce the power it is truly capable of. The work required to adjust and modify the

distributor is minimal in relation to the possible power gains that can easily be achieved.

Up until the mid 1970s, nearly all engines were fitted with an ignition system that had contact breaker points. During the next ten years manufacturers changed over to, or offered as options, engines that were equipped with electronic ignition. During the changeover period some cars were equipped with points-type ignitions and some with electronic ignitions. By the mid-1980s, however, virtually no engines were being fitted with points and, by the mid-1990s, virtually no new engines had a distributor.

Modern ignition systems do not have a distributor as such, instead they usually have a cylinder block-mounted sensor and segments on the flywheel or flexplate or a front-mounted sensor and a 'trigger wheel' with one missing segment or tooth to accurately pinpoint the position of the crankshaft, and this information is relayed to the ECU (Electronic Control Unit) which controls ignition events. Sometimes each sparkplug has its own coil (fixed to the top of the plug) or the coils are housed in a 'coil pack' which is fixed to the engine or on the car's body. Some engines use a different system again, which has one coil with two high tension spark plug wires coming out of it firing two cylinders together. Each coil discharges once every revolution of the engine, though only one cylinder is on the compression stroke, and, because this cylinder is the only one in this condition, nearly all of the available spark discharges into this cylinder. This system is called 'wasted spark.'

To alter the characteristics of these later ignition systems which are part of an engine management system, an alternative modified ECU or programmable ECU is required. This book does not cover ECU controlled,

distributorless ignition systems.

Today there are still thousands of high-performance engines which use a distributor with points or a pickup and electronic module system. The aim of this book is to allow the setting up (and altering where necessary) of distributor-type ignition systems to ensure that the best possible spark is delivered to the tip of the sparkplug at the best possible time. There is little information in this book concerning how ignition systems actually work: it's intended to be a tune-up and uprating guide for distributor-type ignition systems that are being used in a high-performance application.

All ignition systems need a minimum of 12.5-12.8 volts to operate correctly, and this means having a charging system that puts 13.2-14.2 volts across the battery when the engine is running. A good battery which is warm and fully charged can, in fact, hold 13-14 volts. The idea of not fitting an alternator to a competition engine or any high-performance engine and, instead, just using a large capacity battery is not well founded, and is most definitely **not** recommended. Small alternators that put out plenty of amps and take a minimum of engine power to drive them are readily available, such as the Nippon Denso 100211 type, which is very compact and available in 35 and 45 amp outputs. These alternators are available new or rebuilt from car spares and auto-electrical shops. They are found on Daihatsu Charades (100211-6790/4080-45 amp) and Komatsu diggers (100211-1661-35 amp). They cut in and produce power at 800-900rpm, that's alternator rpm, and produce 13.8-14.2 volts at this rpm and above. They can be 'geared' one-to-one to the crankshaft for most engines. This will mean having an aluminium pulley specially made for the alternator which is the same diameter as the pulley on the crankshaft that drives it. Sometimes the alternator pulley can be larger; it just depends on idle rpm, what the power demand will be when the engine's in its application, and what the maximum engine rpm will be. All manner of alternators are available from aftermarket sources, such as PAW, Summit or Jeg's, etc., in the USA. In the UK, try Nick Beere of Ark Racing at www.arkracing.com, info@arkracing.com or 01902 602881.

The advantages of having an alternator fitted certainly outweigh the disadvantages of extra weight and the slight amount of engine power consumed by the unit.

Alternator output needs to be checked frequently (by placing a voltmeter across the battery terminals with just the ignition switched on, and then taking another reading when the engine is running).

IGNITION TIMING THEORY

Ignition firing occurs within a very narrow range of degrees of crankshaft rotation within the 720 degree total cycle of a four-stroke engine. The vast majority of production engines have never have less than 2 degrees before top dead centre of static ignition timing, or more than 36 degrees before top dead centre of total ignition timing. Some standard production engines have had more than 36 degrees of total ignition timing, up to 40 or even 44 degrees, for example, but there haven't been many. Without doubt, the most common amounts of ignition timing found in standard production engines are 4-6 degrees of static ignition timing before top dead centre, and 28-36 degrees of total ignition timing before top dead centre. To cover the total range of ignition timing requirements for the vast majority of standard production engines made since 1960, the area of interest for ignition firing purposes is between 2 degrees before top dead centre and 36 degrees before top dead centre on the

compression stroke of the engine.

The customary crankshaft degree markings seen on engines and universally used by everyone for ignition timing can be directly related to the position of the rising piston crown on the compression stroke just before top dead centre. If you take the average stroke engine as being about 3.000in/76.0mm, it's quite easy to see via a diagram just how small the area of ignition occupies in the four-stroke cycle. In spite of this very small area of operation and applicable piston travel, the correct timing of the ignition is absolutely vital to the power production of any engine:

• At 35 degrees before top dead centre the piston crown is 0.375in/9.50mm away from the top of the cylinder
• At 30 degrees before top dead centre the piston crown is 0.270in/6.8mm away from the top of the cylinder
• At 25 degrees before top dead centre the piston crown is 0.195in/4.9mm away

from the top of the cylinder
• At 20 degrees before top dead centre the piston crown is 0.120in/3.0mm away from the top of the cylinder
• At 15 degrees before top dead centre the piston crown is 0.080in/2.0mm away from the top of the cylinder
• At 10 degrees before top dead centre the piston crown is 0.040in/1.0mm away from the top of the cylinder
• At 5 degrees before top dead centre the piston crown is 0.016in/0.4mm away from the top of the cylinder

To expand this, an engine with a 4.000in/101.5mm stroke has the piston crown about 0.450in/11.5mm away from the top of the cylinder at 35 degrees before top dead centre. An engine with a 2.500in/63.5mm stroke has the piston crown about 0.280in/7.1mm away from the top of the cylinder at 35 degrees before top dead centre. Irrespective of the stroke, if you take the common range of strokes used and look at their

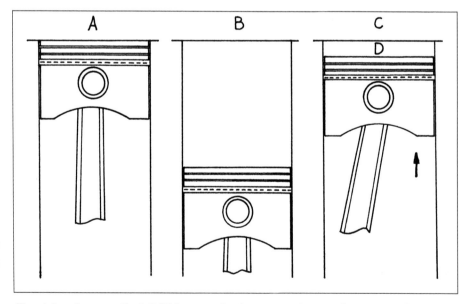

The piston shown on the left (A) is at top dead centre, or the top of the stroke. The piston as shown in the centre (B) is at bottom dead centre, or the bottom of the stroke. The piston on the right (C) is rising as indicated by the direction of the arrow. The top of the piston (crown) is shown at 35 crankshaft degrees before top dead centre. The region where ignition takes place (D) shows just how close the piston crown is to the top of the cylinder at 35 degrees before top dead centre.

35 degree before top dead centre points, the distances from the top of the cylinders are from 0.280in/7.1mm to 0.450in/11.5mm, and this most definitely shows the basic trend for all engines.

Most standard production engines will start easily with between 2-6 degrees of static ignition timing, and idle with this amount of ignition timing at between 600-900rpm. This means that the ignition is going to be firing on average at anything from 0.004in to 0.040in/0.01-1.0mm before the rising piston crown reaches top dead centre (i.e. the piston crown is not very far down the bore). At idle, the throttle is virtually closed and the amount of air mixed with fuel entering the engine is just enough to support correct combustion. A correct air/fuel mixture entering an engine and insufficient ignition timing will result in a 'heavy' sounding engine, while a correct air/fuel mixture and an ideal amount of ignition timing will result in a 'light' sounding engine. If too much ignition timing is present, the idle speed will start to slow and the idle will become rough. What this means is that you can have too little or too much ignition timing at an acceptable idle speed in an engine. Most engines idle best over a 1-2 degree range so if, for example an engine idles perfectly with 6 or 8 degrees of ignition timing, it won't idle quite as well at 4 or 10 degrees. This factor makes picking the optimum amount of ignition timing for any particular engine fairly easy.

It's a known fact that engines produce their maximum torque at maximum 'charge density'; that is, the most air that can be got into the cylinder in any one inlet cycle in any part of the rpm range. This is all related to camshaft timing, inlet valves, inlet port sizes and shape, and inlet manifold, etc. (volumetric efficiency). The rpm point of maximum torque, which is often a 1000rpm-wide band, such as 2200-3200rpm with the absolute 'peak' being

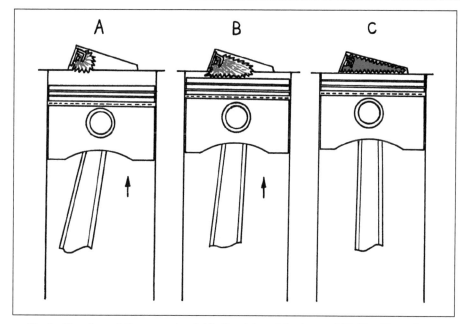

The ignition fires at the correct point in the rising piston's travel (A). The 'flame front' spreads from the point of ignition through the compressed charge, and the still compressing charge (B). The whole of the charge has been exposed to 'flame' at the point of top dead centre (piston stops) as much as it's possible to do so with it now squeezed into the combustion chamber (C). The increasing combustion pressure now pushes the piston downwards (power stroke) as the piston moves down from top dead centre. Consider this to be what happens with optimum ignition. The combustion pressure is still just active as late as 55 degrees before bottom dead centre, but most exhaust valves of even the most mild camshaft equipped engines will have started to open by this stage.

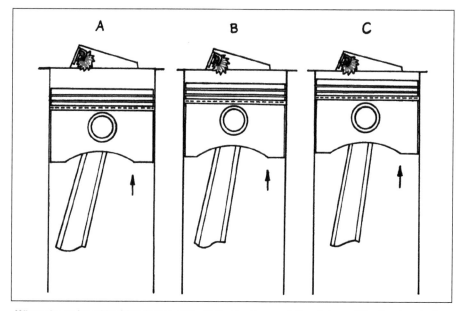

When the point of ignition is too early or 'over advanced' the piston will be too low in the cylinder (A). B shows the piston timed exactly right for optimum ignition. When there is insufficient ignition timing, the piston is too close to the top of the cylinder (C).

2700rpm, is going to require a specific amount of ignition timing to achieve it. 1-2 degrees either side of the optimum amount of ignition timing will mean a power loss.

If insufficient ignition timing is set into an engine the maximum torque will not be realised because the ignition will be too late. When this happens the combustion pressure won't have time to build up to the maximum possible and push the descending piston down as well as it might on the power stroke. The engine will run well enough, but not as good as it could. Conversely, if too much ignition timing is set into an engine, that's the rising piston crown too far away from top dead centre when the ignition is fired, the combustion pressure builds up too quickly and starts to work against the still rising, but slowing piston, and the engine torque will be reduced because of this factor. It's a reasonably fine line between having it right and having it wrong.

In general, to produce maximum torque, engines require ignition timings in the region of 28-36 degrees before top dead centre (that's a rising piston crown on the compression stroke and the ignition firing anything from 0.250-0.375in/6.3mm to 0.500in/12.6mm before the piston crown reaches the top of the cylinder). After the point of maximum torque has been reached, the charge density slowly reduces, as does the amount of torque being developed, as the rpm increases.

The amount of ignition timing an engine has after the point of maximum torque has been reached is largely academic; meaning, if the ignition timing is further advanced, it doesn't tend to make any difference to the power output because there isn't the same 'charge density' present in the engine. Some engines respond to a couple of degrees more total ignition timing at the point of maximum power, while others require a

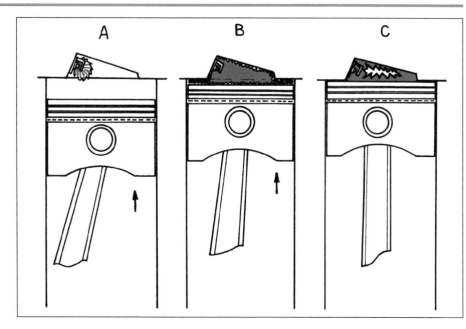

With the ignition fired too early (A), the combustion pressure rise is too rapid, and very high pressure is present before the (slowing) piston reaches the top of the cylinder (B). The already expanding pressure is then forced into the confines of the combustion chamber (C), and this is when 'pinking' will be heard (over-advanced ignition timing).

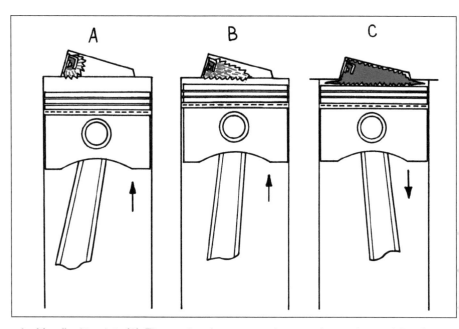

Ignition fired too late (A). The combustion pressure increase is too slow and the 'flame front' doesn't spread through the still compressing charge (B) before top dead centre is reached. The point where most of the charge has been exposed to 'flame' is after top dead centre and the piston is already starting to descend the cylinder (C). The increase in cylinder pressure is not quite quick enough to cause optimum down-force to be exerted on the piston crown, so optimum engine performance is not achieved (retarded ignition timing).

slight reduction in total ignition timing at maximum power (a couple of degrees). Incorporating a few more degrees into a mechanical advance distributor is possible, but reducing the ignition timing in the sort of distributor under discussion here is not. This is where modern programmable electronic ignition systems are excellent; you can put in any number degrees of ignition timing at any point in the rpm range.

The amount of ignition timing for optimum idle speed smoothness is different from that required to produce maximum torque, which is why distributors have a mechanical advance mechanism incorporated into them. There are two distinct regimes in operation in a four-stroke engine, and the mechanical advance is there to effectively join the two together as smoothly and as effectively as possible.

Note that the idea of advancing the ignition from the ideal idle amount of ignition timing to the ideal total amount of ignition timing as quickly as is possible, conducive to there being no 'pinking' under load, is a well founded principle. There are a few terms for 'pinking' such as 'pinging' or 'rattling.' The term used throughout this book is 'pinking' for no other reason than that's the term I've always used.

As the rpm increases from idle, the ignition timing advances too, so that between the engine idle speed and the point of maximum torque, the ignition timing is advanced at the required rate (neither too slow nor too fast). If the ignition timing is advanced too quickly, the engine will hesitate, or 'kick-back,' as the ignition is firing too early and the combustion pressure increase will be too rapid and will work against the rising piston. If the ignition timing is advanced too slowly, the optimum combustion 'pressure rise' required to develop best possible engine performance and engine acceleration will not be present, and the

engine's acceleration rate will be slower than it could be.

To get the ignition timing advancing at the correct rate (controlled by the advance springs) is a reasonably exacting process, but not that difficult to achieve.

With an engine dyno, it's very easy to work out the precise maximum torque and power ignition timing requirements, and it's very easy to ascertain when in the rpm range the maximum amount of ignition timing needs to be present.

With the engine set at a conservative amount of ignition timing, such as 28 degrees before top dead centre, a power run is done on the dyno, readings taken, the ignition timing altered (increased by 2 degrees), and another power run taken. Advancing the ignition timing continues in this manner until the measured peak torque starts to reduce. The amount of ignition timing it takes to develop maximum torque might be precisely 35 degrees before top dead centre, with the maximum torque starting to reduce with 36 degrees before top dead centre. The engine has to be taken past the optimum setting of total ignition timing and register a small reduction in torque, such as 2-10 foot pounds, depending on the size of the engine, small engine small (2 foot pounds) reduction large engine bigger reduction (10 foot pounds) for example, to find the peak. The further the ignition timing is taken past the peak, the bigger the reduction in torque.

The printout that you'll receive following your dyno session will give the torque values from the point in the rpm the testing starts until the testing cycle ceases. If the advance mechanism springs in the distributor are changed for 'lighter' ones and the value of the torque changes for the better on the 'low' side of the torque curve, then this is a clear indication that the engine responded to the ignition timing being advanced at a

faster rate. Continue reducing the spring tension but, as a general rule, never have the ignition timing fully advanced earlier than 2500rpm. If, on the other hand, the torque value drops, it's a fair indication that the ignition timing is being advanced too quickly, so go back to the original springs and increase the tension slightly above them to see if the torque values improve. If they don't, go back to the original springs. If the values improve, keep increasing the spring tensions until there's no improvement and then go back to the previous springs.

On top of the total amount of ignition timing you can add approximately 10 degrees for the vacuum advance for roadgoing engines. However, the vacuum advance will only be in operation when the engine is generating vacuum, and this can only happen on a partial throttle, such as when driving on a motorway/highway/freeway at a set cruising speed. The lighter the throttle being used, the more vacuum advance there will be present, up to the maximum the particular mechanism can give. The vacuum advance plays no part in developing maximum torque and maximum power. The maximum amount of ignition timing that roadgoing engines use under these conditions is approximately 35-45 degrees with the vacuum advance system fully operational and at the maximum permissible setting. The standard amounts of vacuum advance built into the vacuum canister are generally sufficient and correct for the particular engine, and no one ever modifies them as it just isn't necessary to do so. The values of vacuum canisters does vary a bit, though, and it's possible to buy one that gives more or less ignition timing advance when the engine is operating under vacuum. The reason an engine can tolerate this amount of ignition timing is because the engine is operating under partial throttle and 'low charge density' conditions, which means the engine won't 'pink.' If an engine does 'pink' under vacuum advance only, it's likely that the vacuum canister is allowing too much advanced ignition timing for the amount of vacuum being generated. Check to see if there is a different calibrated vacuum canister available for your distributor. The instant the throttle is opened the engine is not under vacuum and the mechanism retards before any damage can be done (pre-ignition). As a result of this, all roadgoing engines need to have vacuum advance fitted to them if maximum fuel economy is to be achieved. Racing engines, on the other hand, don't and shouldn't have an operative vacuum advance system fitted to them.

Chapter 1
Modified engines often need higher ignition timing settings

When manufacturers design and build engines they make them to suit a wide range of operating conditions and to suit all types of driving style. There is really nothing they can leave out of the equation; their engines have to be suitable for every driving style imaginable and vehicle use. Engines have to deliver good fuel economy, pull from low rpm in high gears, power cars that tow loaded trailers, have a turn of speed suitable for long distance travel, require minimal maintenance, start from hot or cold instantly, and so on.

However, once the application changes, so can some of the criteria because such an engine isn't going to be laboured, and so on. A modified engine is seldom expected to operate smoothly and give good power between 500rpm and 2000rpm as many standard engines do. Modified engines have almost always had a camshaft change and cylinder head modifications to improve the power output of the engine. A dead smooth, vibration-free idle speed

of 750rpm is relinquished for camshaft related idle speed roughness of varying degrees, and an idle speed which is often between 1000rpm-1500rpm. Instead of smooth motive power being available from 750rpm through 2250rpm, the engine produces less power under 2250rpm, but much more power when the camshaft 'smoothes out' and starts to 'work.'

Modifications of the cylinder head and camshaft duration play a part, but it is mainly camshaft overlap which causes the major change to the amount of static or idle speed ignition timing that a given engine will require.

With the average standard camshaft fitted to a standard engine, the likely idle speed ignition timing required could be anything from 2 to 6 degrees before top dead centre (BTDC). Such an engine will usually idle and accelerate smoothly, and possibly quite slowly, without any 'pinking' at all.

If on such an engine the ignition timing was advanced at the 750rpm idle

speed from the listed 2-4 degrees before top dead centre to 12-14 degrees before top dead centre, the idle might well become slightly rough and unacceptable. If the ignition timing was left like this, the engine might 'pink' a considerable amount when accelerating from low rpm.

On the other hand, the engine might also respond extremely well to the increased ignition timing, and go a lot better throughout the entire rpm range and also deliver much improved fuel economy (10-20% not being unknown). Some engines are factory set with very conservative amounts of ignition timing, and it's done like this in part so that the engine will do anything a driver might subject it to. Engine manufacturers have to cover every imaginable eventuality, including the ones that they wouldn't even dream of as being possible. We in the performance car world, on the other hand, do not have to take into consideration the near impossible.

In just about all instances, the number of degrees of ignition timing that any engine, standard or otherwise, will respond best to for idling purposes will be between 8-16 degrees before top dead centre. Few engines need less than 8 and few require more than 16, but some do require more, such as up to to 24 degrees BTDC (petrol/gasoline burning engines that is).

Fitting a modified cylinder head amplifies the camshaft characteristics as the ports flow better than standard (usually): on this basis the cylinder head is tied in with a camshaft change.

With a change to a high-performance camshaft, the overlap (that's the total number of crankshaft degrees that the opening inlet valve and the closing exhaust valve are off their seats together) plays a major part in the volumetric efficiency of the engine at low rpm. So, where, before the engine

idled quite satisfactorily at 600rpm it might now require 1200rpm to achieve acceptable idle smoothness or require this minimum amount of idle speed to simply keep running. The engine will also require a certain number of revs to be reached before it runs smoothly. When the camshaft events reach a certain speed, operational smoothness is achieved and the camshaft can be considered to be 'working' and the engine will deliver worthwhile power.

In the period before the camshaft is 'working,' the modified engine is not as efficient as the standard engine would be. The volumetric efficiency (cylinder filling) of the standard engine is better than the modified engine at low engine rpm. The end result of this is that the modified engine needs more initial ignition timing than a standard engine.

A small point to bear in mind is that, of course, the standard engine is turning over at 750rpm at idle, not 1000-1500rpm (2-6 degrees perhaps). The overall point is that engines modified for high performance almost always require advanced ignition timing compared to its standard counterpart, but not necessarily more total ignition timing, so it isn't simply a case of increasing the idle speed ignition timing by loosening the distributor clamp and turning the distributor body to a more advanced position, tightening the clamp, and expecting the total amount of ignition timing to then be correct. The engine will almost certainly be grossly 'over advanced' at the point of maximum torque if you do just this. Too much total ignition timing reduces engine performance and can wreck engines.

Chapter 2
Static & idle speed ignition timing settings

STATIC IGNITION TIMING

This is the amount of ignition timing an engine has when stationary, and what it will actually fire up with when it's turned over by the starter motor. Starter motors can usually cold start an engine from 60rpm, but on average they will turn over an engine at about 80-100rpm. Strong starters, like geared ones, are able to turn over an engine at up to 120-150rpm. It's also the minimum amount of ignition timing the engine will ever have when running. The rate of ignition timing advance of the engine from this point on is controlled by the two small springs of the 'mechanical advance mechanism.'

The amount of static ignition timing is determined by two things: the amount of ignition timing (advance) that the starter motor can successfully turn over, and the amount of ignition timing the engine idles best at. There is no point in having so much ignition timing that starting the engine is difficult. There is always a maximum, sensible amount

of ignition timing possible for starting purposes. Start with 8 degrees which is an amount of static advance which all engines are virtually guaranteed to start on, warm up the engine and try starting it again, this time with 10, 12, 14 and 16 degrees of ignition timing. Expect possible starting problems (kicking back) at anything above 14-16 degrees, but it has to be said that many engines start without any trouble at all with 18 or 20 degrees of static ignition timing. Modern starters have a lot of power, and will often turn over any engine, irrespective of the compression ratio, etc., provided the ignition timing isn't too outrageous. It's the older design of starter which might have problems consistently turning over an engine which has 12-14 degrees of static ignition timing set into it.

Find out by test what amount of static ignition timing causes the starter motor difficulty in turning over the engine; you can't afford to exceed this amount of static ignition timing at any later stage so you do need to know it.

Keep in mind that the use of a good capacity, fully charged battery is vital for starting purposes, and that anything less can be the cause of poor starter motor performance and an invalid test.

Note that while it's very easy to check the static ignition timing with a points-type distributor, it's not so easy with an electronic one. With a points-type distributor and an engine that has a degree marked crankshaft pulley or crankshaft damper, all you have to do is slowly turn over the engine using a spanner or socket on the crankshaft nut until the points just open, and read off the degree markings. This might seem a crude method but, on average, it is accurate to within a degree and a bit of practice makes perfect. The electronic distributor isn't quite so easy.

IDLE SPEED IGNITION TIMING

This is the amount of ignition timing that causes the engine to idle at its best. That's the smoothest possible even beat and lightest exhaust pulsing at a sensible idle speed for its state of tune (usually denoted by the camshaft degrees of duration). The optimum idle speed ignition timing has to be found by test because there will be some variation between engines of the same type even because of compression ratios, etc. With a distributor, finding the optimum idle speed ignition timing is quite easily achieved by advancing and retarding the ignition timing (with the vacuum pipe disconnected, of course) with the engine idling not too fast, and commensurate with the state of tune.

Once the idle speed ignition timing has been found, the engine is switched off and then restarted. If, when the engine is turned over on the starter, it fires up with no trouble at all, the base amount of static and idle speed ignition timing will be one and the same. If, on the other hand, the starter is obviously under strain, the idle speed ignition timing and the static ignition timing will need to be different. If the starter won't turn the engine over easily and start it, there will have to be an amount of static ignition timing for starting and another amount for the idle. As a result, the static and idle speed ignition timing can either be the same or they can be different.

Depending on the level of engine modifications, compression ratio, octane rating of the fuel being used, etc., high-performance-orientated engines will need anything from 10-16 degrees of idle speed ignition timing and, in some cases, up to 20 degrees of idle speed ignition timing. Many standard engines can also use a higher ignition timing figure than the standard recommended amount, so it isn't just modified engines that can have this testing regime applied to them. Each individual engine has to be checked and tested to find out what it will require to deliver optimum idle smoothness and power for immediate off idle response.

Note that some engines are going to require 8 or 10 degrees of idle speed ignition timing as opposed to 10-16 degrees, but it's unlikely that any performance orientated engine will require less than 8 degrees of idle speed ignition timing.

Virtually all engines will start with up to 15 degrees of static ignition timing, and few will require less than 10 degrees or more than 15 degrees, so there isn't usually a problem with this aspect of ignition tuning in the area up to 15 degrees of ignition timing for starting or idle speed purposes. Any problems that do arise can be solved quite easily, but more work is involved when the static and the idle speed ignition timing amounts are different. It's after 15 degrees BTDC of static ignition timing that some starter motors are not able to function correctly, though there is a way around this problem.

As a guide to how much idle speed ignition timing you can expect an engine to need, consider the following table.

270 degree cam: 8-12 degrees BTDC
280 degree cam: 10-14 degrees BTDC
290 degree cam: 12-16 degrees BTDC
300 degree cam: 14-18 degrees BTDC
310 degree cam: 16-20 degrees BTDC

IDLE IGNITION TIMING

The first thing that needs to be done is to work out just how much idle speed ignition timing a particular engine will require. In the first instance, 10 degrees of static ignition timing is going to be sufficient to start any engine. In fact, there isn't much point in setting the static ignition timing at anything less. Electronic ignition systems initially might need a bit of guesswork when it comes to positioning the distributor, but once the engine has started the ignition timing can be set with a strobe light to 10 degrees.

Reminder! Always check that the tip of the rotor arm is placed adjacent to the correct post of the distributor cap, but slightly to one side of the post for ignition firing. The reason for this is that it's a requirement for the tip of the rotor to always be 'covering' the post when the spark is discharged. This is why the tip of the rotor arm is always at least two or three times as wide as the post. As the ignition timing is mechanically advanced, the rotor changes its effective position (moves forwards or advances in the direction of the distributor's rotation). The sweep of the rotor arm tip from the static advance position to the fully mechanically advanced, and the vacuum advance mechanism fully advanced position if fitted, must see the distributor cap post opposed by the tip of the rotor arm (full radial contact but with a gap between the two components), the firing order is correct, and the engine is on the compression stroke for number 1 cylinder. Check that the inlet and exhaust valves are shut on number one cylinder, and that the rotor arm is indeed pointing at the right post of the distributor cap. More than one engine has been found to have a high speed misfire because the rotor arm tip is not in line with the posts (no longer opposing the posts, and even moved past the posts)! Also a huge number of engines prove difficult to start because the basics simply have not been thoroughly checked.

With the engine running and using 10 degrees of ignition timing, the ignition timing is advanced from this position to find the smoothest idle/highest rpm point. The engine is then switched off and restarted. If the engine starts fine, and there is no 'kickback,' then setting the ignition timing is going to be quite straightforward.

It is possible for the ideal number of ignition timing degrees to be too much for the starter motor, and the static ignition timing will have to be retarded to allow the engine to be started. For example, if the starter motor will allow 14 degrees of ignition advance with easy starting, but for optimum engine idle smoothness the engine requires 16 degrees of ignition timing, many people will just settle for 14 degrees of static advance and let the engine idle with slightly less advance than it really needs. This is quite acceptable because it is well below the usable rpm range and can't possibly affect the engine performance where it really matters, although it can affect 'clean running' at low rpm (that's the first 500rpm up from the idle speed).

If the starter motor will only allow 12 degrees of static ignition timing for successful starting, but the engine needs a minimum of 16 degrees of idle speed advance at 1200rpm to attain a smooth idle, the ignition timing is set for 12 degrees before top dead centre and the ignition advance springs are set for tension to allow the mechanical advance to start working much earlier than it would otherwise. This way, the engine has 12 degrees of static advance when stationary, and 12 degrees of advance when the starter motor is turning the engine over at the usual 60-90rpm, but the advance mechanism springs allow the mechanical advance to start to advance at, say, 800rpm, so that at 1200rpm the mechanical advance has moved 4 degrees. Getting this right is often easier said than done, because one of the advance springs is going to have to be quite weak and perfectly matched to the requirements. This is where a good range of distributor advance springs from a variety of distributors comes into the equation.

IDLE SPEEDS

The camshaft has a huge bearing on what the actual idle speed is, and every engine is going to be different. For these tests the idle speed is set as low and as smooth as is practical. The range of idle

speeds in relation to camshaft duration and overlap is as follows, but note that, if the idle speed is set very much above the recommended settings, the outcome will not be correct for good idling and acceleration response.

270 degree cam: 600-800rpm
280 degree cam: 800-1000rpm
290 degree cam: 1000-1200rpm
300 degree cam: 1200-1400rpm
310 degree cam: 1300-1500rpm

The idle ignition timing figure can be ascertained before the original distributor is modified. However, unless you have had previous experience with the engine concerned and know what the idle speed and the total ignition timing requirements are, an original specification distributor of some sort will have to be fitted to the engine and used to find out what the optimum starting, idle speed and total ignition timing requirements are.

Caution! When testing using a standard distributor which has a lot of mechanical advance built into it (more than 10 degrees in the distributor or more than 20 crankshaft degrees) no attempt should be made to run the engine over 2000-2500rpm. The best policy by far is to find and fit a distributor which has 9-10 degrees of mechanical ignition timing advance built into it (which equates to 18-20 crankshaft degrees). This way there is no risk of sustaining any engine damage through error.

Note that a distributor spindle of a four-stroke engine turns at half the rotational speed of the crankshaft, so when you're talking about distributor degrees and crankshaft degrees of ignition timing this factor has to be taken into consideration. Distributor degrees and crankshaft ignition timing degrees are not the same, crankshaft degrees are always twice that of the distributor. All ignition timing is done in crankshaft degrees, so the distributor

This very early (1961-1963) Autolite small block Ford V8 distributor cam-plate has the number 10 stamped on the 'cam plate,' signifying that 10 degrees of mechanical advance is built in, equating to 20 degrees of ignition timing as measured on the crankshaft. This is a very desirable distributor to have if you're using a modified small block Ford V8 engine because it allows for 14-16 degrees of static ignition timing and 34-36 degree total ignition timing with only the advance mechanism springs to be changed to suit the application.

degrees need to be doubled to equate to it. A distributor which has 10 degrees of advance built into it equates to 20 degrees of ignition timing as measured with a strobe light on the crankshaft. With distributors and ignition timing you need to understand the situation and learn to work between the two factors.

The problem is that if the distributor has 6 degrees of static ignition timing, and 15 degrees of mechanical advance built into it, which is going to show up as 30 degrees of ignition timing at the crankshaft, the total amount of ignition timing is going to be 36 degrees BTDC. If you then start increasing the static/idle speed to 10-16 degrees of ignition timing or more, it's not impossible to end up with excessive ignition timing. For example, if such a distributor was set for 16 degrees of static/idle speed advance, the engine would have 46 degrees of total ignition timing, which would be far too much. The solution is to find a standard distributor which has less mechanical advance built in it. Fortunately, most engines have at least 5 or 6 different factory amounts of mechanical advance. The distributors fitted to the small block Ford V8 engines, for example, had 10 through 17 degrees of mechanical advance on average built into them, equating to 20 degrees through 34 degrees of ignition timing as measured on the crankshaft with a strobe light). To achieve 36 degrees of total ignition timing with a 17 degree distributor (34 crankshaft degrees), the static ignition timing would be set at 2 degrees before top dead centre. Some engine manufacturers even made distributors which had 9-10 degrees of mechanical advance built into them (equating to 18-20 degrees of ignition timing on the crankshaft). This is the lowest amount of distributor mechanical advance you are ever likely to find in a stock type distributor. These are the most desirable stock type distributors as they require the least amount of work to prepare them for high performance or racing engine use.

Scrap-yards, swap meets, auto-jumbles and the like are excellent places to find such things. **Caution!** Distributors are not all the same in this respect! It may take a bit of searching to find the 'right' distributor. More obscure distributors will often have to be modified because there aren't secondhand ones available.

In the majority of instances, a distributor which will be suitable for many standard engines and the vast majority of modified engines will not need to have more than 18-22 crankshaft degrees of ignition timing advance built into it. It's always better to work with a distributor which has an amount of mechanical ignition timing advance which is going to be close to the final requirement. For example, if an engine requires 16 degrees of static/idle speed ignition timing and 36 degrees of total ignition timing, a distributor which has 10 degrees of mechanical advance built into it which gives 20 degrees of ignition timing on the crankshaft is required. This 10/20 degree amount of mechanical advance of the ignition timing covers a huge number of engine requirements. If, on the other hand, an engine needs 12 degrees of static/idle speed advance and 38 degrees of total ignition timing built in the distributor, that's 13 degrees of mechanical advance built into the distributor (which equates to 26 degrees of ignition advance on the crankshaft as measured with a strobe light), and the more common standard distributors might be suitable.

IDENTIFYING THE AMOUNT OF MECHANICAL ADVANCE

The number of degrees of mechanical advance is almost always stamped on the cam-plate.

Note that the term 'cam-plate' applies to points type distributors and the distributor cam which opens and closes the points. The name remained, even with the universal adoption of electronic means to replace points. Instead of distributors having a cam, they now have a 'reluctor' or 'chopper plate' that fits over the original cam if a points to electronic conversion is being used. On later electronic distributors, what was called the 'cam-plate' is more likely to be referred to as the 'advance plate' or 'advance mechanism plate.' The total range of distributors built in mechanical amounts of advance in degrees, as made by all manufactures, usually sees cam-plates with 9, 9½, 10, 10½, 11, 11½, 12, 12½, 13, 13½, 14, 14½, 15, 15½, 16, 16½ and 17 markings on them. This means 18, 19, 20, 21, 22, 23, 24, 25, 26, 27, 28, 29, 30, 31, 32, 33 and 34 degrees of total ignition timing degrees on the crankshaft. Not all manufactures make this sort of range for an engine because they don't need to, they make and use a range that suits the individual engine requirements. Some 'cam-plates' don't have numbers stamped on them, and you have to resort to measuring the actual distributor degrees, as covered later in the book, and work out how much mechanical ignition timing advance it has built into it.

It's actually not very often that an existing 'cam-plate' has to be altered to reduce the number of mechanical ignition timing degrees a distributor has. It's usually much easier to find a distributor of the right type (model) than start altering existing componentry. Consequently, it does pay to collect distributors of the type your engine has because, not only will it give you spare parts, one might just have the right amount of mechanical advance for your application.

Chapter 3
Estimating total advance settings

A wide range of combustion chamber shapes have been used by engine manufacturers over the years, and the overall burning efficiency of the particular combustion chamber shape determines the total amount of ignition advance that will be required to produce maximum torque through to the point of maximum power. The accompanying photo sequence covers the basic range of combustion chamber shapes that are most usually found. Match as closely as possible the combustion chamber shape of your engine's cylinder head to one of the pictures and use the number of total degrees listed with each photograph as a guide to what amount of total advance will most likely suit your engine.

While you don't have to categorise your engine's likely total ignition timing needs, it's helpful so that you're close to the required amount when starting the tune up procedure knowing that you'll be, on average, within 2-3 degrees of the final setting and be doing the tune up work without risk of engine damage

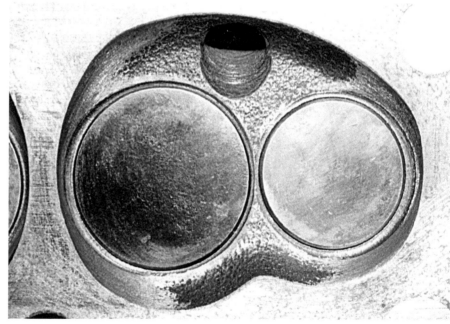

Heart-shaped combustion chamber – 33-35 degrees of total ignition timing. Note that the sparkplug is located to one side of the combustion chamber.

through being outrageously out in your settings. The following photos and amounts of total ignition timing are a good guide to the basic requirements.

Caution! Note that every ignition timing setting must be checked thoroughly with all aspects of the engine tune taken into consideration (mixture

21

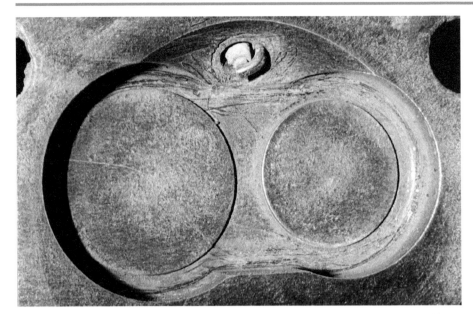

Bathtub combustion chamber – 32 to 36 degrees of total ignition timing. Note that the sparkplug is located to one side of the combustion chamber.

Hemispherical combustion chamber – 34 to 38 degrees of total ignition timing generally although some applications will go to an absolute maximum of 44 degrees of total advance. Note that the sparkplug is located as near to the centre of the combustion chamber as is possible.

strength, engine temperature, and so on) before the engine is subjected to wide open throttle conditions. Serious engine damage can result if too much total ignition timing is used. Conversely, if not enough ignition timing is used, your engine may never ever go as well as it should, and it may also run extremely hot while doing so. Retarded ignition timing engines are frequently very difficult to keep cool.

There are several reasons why racing engines, for example, end up having their ignition timings retarded, and one is that the engine has too much compression for the RON and MON octane rating of the fuel being used. What very often happens is that an engine which has, say, 12.0:1-12.5:1 compression, is run on 97-98 RON octane pump fuel when, in actual fact, 10.5:1-11.0:1 would be a much more

suitable amount of compression for this sort of octane rating fuel. You can set an engine like this to run quite well in these adverse conditions, however, by reducing the amount of idle speed and total advance ignition timing, and by slowing the rate of the advance of the ignition timing. If the engine has a compression ratio which is matched to the octane rating of the fuel, the ignition timing might be 15 degrees at idle, and 35 degrees total ignition timing at maximum torque. The ignition timing advance rate from 15 degrees to 35 degrees BTDC might happen between 1300-3300rpm. What you end up doing is reducing the degrees of ignition timing until the 'pinking' stops, and increasing the rpm at which maximum ignition advance is reached. To get such an engine to run without 'pinking' and give good performance, the ignition timing at idle might end up at 8 or 9 degrees, and the total ignition timing at 28 or 29

Closed combustion chamber – 36 to 40 degrees of total ignition timing. Note that the sparkplug is located to one side of the combustion chamber and is aimed towards the centre of the inlet valve.

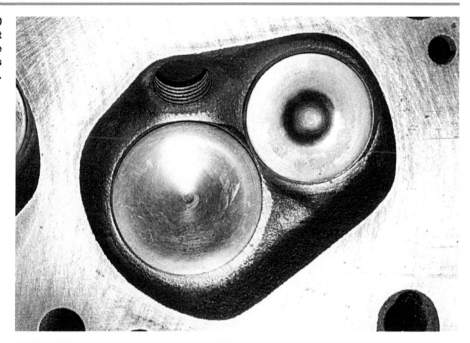

Wedge-type combustion chamber – 36 to 42 degrees of total ignition timing. Note that the sparkplug is located to one side of the combustion chamber and aimed towards the exhaust valve.

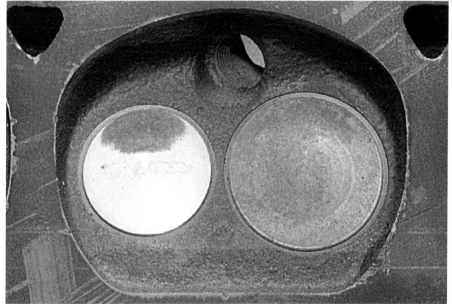

degrees (and the total ignition timing might not be able to be reached until 4000-4500rpm). If this scenario fits your situation expect to have to reduce the overall ignition timing by 5-7 degrees, and slow the rate of advance down accordingly. In many instances the lower compression version of the exact same engine goes better than the higher compression version, and it runs cooler in the process.

If the RON and MON octane rating of the fuel is increased to suit the higher compression ratio, the ignition timing usually needs to be increased to something resembling the settings for the lower compression engine. It will run much better (and cooler) and without any sign of 'pinking.' It's always better to run the amount of compression that suits the octane rating of the fuel being used. In spite of all of this, everyone seems to be into having as high a compression ratio as possible built into their engine, and

that just about always means too much compression for the octane rating of the available fuel which is going to be used.

In many instances, a total amount of ignition timing is used in an engine simply because the owner has heard that someone else has used such an amount. The ignition timing never gets altered from that setting. This is why

these guidelines for total ignition timing need to be taken into consideration so that an estimate of the likely amount of total ignition timing is a known factor, and also to prevent an outrageous amount of timing from being used under any circumstances. Many people have experienced problems with engines and kept advancing the ignition timing in the

Open wedge combustion chamber – 28 to 36 degrees of total ignition timing. Note that the sparkplug is as central as is possible and aimed at the exhaust valve, which is a very desirable feature.

Four-valve, pentroof combustion chamber – 28 to 34 degrees of total ignition timing. Centrally placed sparkplug is ideal.

COMBUSTION CHAMBER SHAPES

Most engines are going to have a total ignition timing requirement of between 28-36 degrees before top dead center (vacuum advance disconnected), with only some hemispherical cylinder headed engines using as much as 36-44 degrees of total ignition timing.

The least amount of ignition timing that allows maximum torque to be developed is the optimum. It is a question of having enough; no more, no less.

If the engine is assembled and you are unsure of the combustion chamber shape, look in a repair manual or go to a breaker's yard or engine machine shop and ask if they have a cylinder head of the appropriate type. Look at the perimeter shape and the position of the sparkplug to determine what sort of combustion chamber your engine has so that you can estimate the total amount of spark advance it is likely to need.

mistaken belief that, if a bit is good, a lot is better. It isn't like that with the total ignition timing.

Once the combustion chamber shape has been roughly categorized and the number of degrees of total advance most likely to be required decided upon, and the engine then tested as described in chapter 12, the objective of the information in this chapter (3) is to get a very close estimation of the optimum total amount of ignition timing for your particular engine, so that no massive and potentially costly errors are made due to over-advancing the ignition timing, and that the maximum possible engine efficiency is realised in a reasonable time frame.

Caution! Be aware that some manufacturers use different combustion chamber shapes in what are otherwise identical heads; absolutely correct identification is essential.

Using the four valve, pentroof combustion chamber as an example, the total amount of ignition timing required is usually between 28-34 degrees before top dead centre (BTDC). This range is almost always used for any engine which has this configuration, and won't alter regardless of whether the engine is standard or fully modified because it's the optimum amount of total ignition timing required by the design. Increasing the ignition timing to 36 degrees does not improve the power output any more than reducing the ignition timing to 26 or 24 does. Each engine's total amount of ignition timing needs to be narrowed down to within 1 degree in the listed range.

Compact, wedge-type combustion chamber with the sparkplug aimed towards the exhaust valve uses 34-36 degrees of total ignition timing.

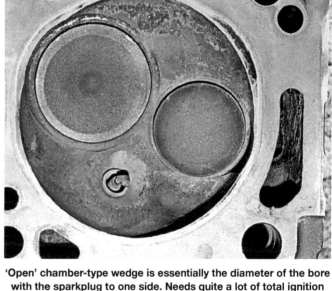

'Open' chamber-type wedge is essentially the diameter of the bore with the sparkplug to one side. Needs quite a lot of total ignition timing, like 38-40 degrees.

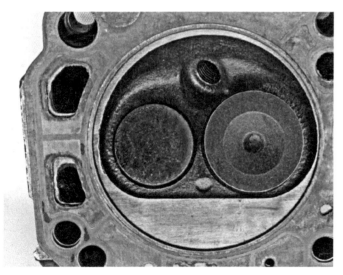

With the head gasket overlaid onto this cylinder head it's quite easy to see the offset of the sparkplug in relation to the bore axis.

C3 Ford V8 racing cylinder head combustion chamber uses 36-38 degrees of total ignition timing.

Gurney-Weslake Ford V8 combustion chamber uses 36-38 degrees of total ignition timing.

Compact wedge combustion chamber uses 34-36 degrees of total ignition timing.

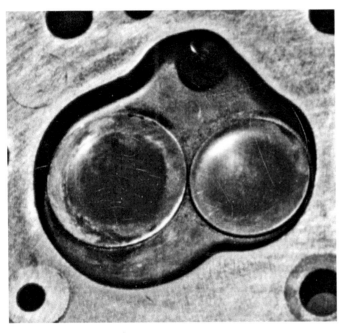

Weslake 1275cc A-Series combustion chamber uses 34-36 degrees of total ignition timing.

Ford V8 Boss 302ci combustion chamber uses 38 degrees of ignition timing.

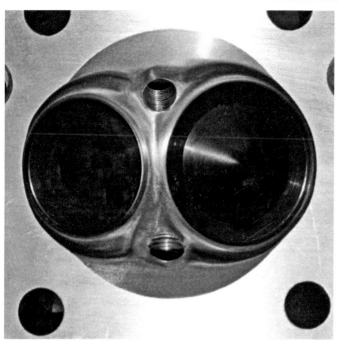

Twin sparkplug modified semi-hemispherical uses 36 degrees of total ignition timing.

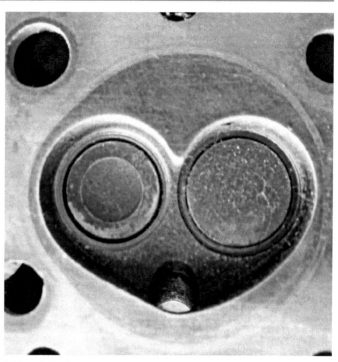

998cc A-Series engine's 'heart-shaped' combustion chamber uses 33-35 degrees of total ignition timing.

SUMMARY

Optimum amounts of total ignition timing vary with engine design, but are narrowed down through performance testing. The optimum amount of ignition timing of all engines can be found by testing, irrespective of what the combustion chamber shape is, what is done to un-shroud the valves, etc., or by planing the cylinder head to increase the compression ratio. Thorough testing results in the optimum amount of ignition timing being found, all things being taken into consideration. For instance, the true hemispherical head engine – such as a Jaguar XK engine – with a piston that does not alter the overall effect of the combustion chamber by offering 'squish' (a piston that is flat-topped or has a slightly raised area in the middle) – will almost always require 38-44 degrees of total ignition timing, with it 'all in' at 3000-3500rpm (depending on the camshaft which alters the point of maximum torque). Engines with this combustion chamber shape frequently 'like' slightly less idle ignition timing (10-12 degrees) and slightly more total ignition timing (38 or more) than do other engines.

The next example is the four valve, pentroof combustion chamber as found in most production car engines these days. These engines will require a maximum of about 32 degrees of total ignition timing on average, with the range of 28-34 degrees covering all engines of this cylinder head design, the point of maximum torque varying depending on the type of camshaft used.

All other engine designs are effectively somewhere in-between the two examples given on the basis of ignition timing degrees BTDC. The point of maximum torque does vary, of course, and, while the ignition timing cannot be fully advanced too early in many instances, 2750rpm is very acceptable. This is the earliest virtually any engine could tolerate, although some engines will go down to 2500rpm, but this is pushing the envelope. Consider the very usual range of having the ignition timing 'all in' or fully mechanically advanced as being between 2750 and 3750rpm irrespective of the type of camshafts used.

The situation revolves around the position of the sparkplug in relation to the centre of the bore axis, the distance as a proportion from the sparkplug electrode from one side of the combustion chamber to the other, the overall distance from the sparkplug electrode to all perimeter points of the combustion chamber, and the shape of the top of the piston (dished, flat or raised topped). The four valve per cylinder combustion chamber used in conjunction with a flat-topped piston shapes up to be quite a good system, and this is the current worldwide trend in engines.

Chapter 4
Vacuum advance

A vacuum advance mechanism is an economy device and, for virtually all road applications, it is necessary and should not be removed. What vacuum advance does is to advance the ignition timing when the engine is not under high load. While an engine may require 35 degrees of total ignition timing to produce maximum torque, it will operate with up to another 5-10 degrees of ignition timing (45 degrees of total ignition timing) when under partial loading, such as when cruising down the motorway, and this will cause the engine to deliver better miles per gallon/km per litre. The higher the vacuum being generated by the engine the more ignition timing the vacuum advance will 'put' into the engine. A reasonably powerful car cruising down the motorway at the speed limit with just the driver on board is going to deliver the best possible fuel economy. That same car with six people in it will not do quite as well because the driver will have to have his foot down on the accelerator a bit more and less vacuum will be

being produced and, subsequently, less vacuum-controlled ignition timing. The engine will be under more load and will be using more fuel because of this factor.

On average, manufacturers calibrate the vacuum advance mechanism to advance the ignition timing anything from a maximum of 10 to as much as 15 degrees above the total mechanical amount of ignition timing, and within this amount the 'extra' ignition timing used within this range will be based on the actual loading on the engine.

Take, as an example, a car being driven down a motorway at a constant speed with the engine turning 3500rpm and needing only 10% throttle to do so. The inlet manifold will be under a lot of vacuum with such a small throttle opening so the vacuum advance mechanism will advance the ignition timing via the mechanical link from the vacuum advance diaphragm to the distributor's baseplate. The amount of advance will vary from engine to engine, but consider about 5-10 degrees more

than the total ignition timing to be fair and reasonable for virtually any standard production engine of this type operating under these sort of conditions. The improvement in fuel economy can be as much as 20 per cent and is seldom ever less than 10 percent versus an engine run without vacuum advance.

When this same engine is subjected to load, such as going up a hill, the engine requires more throttle and as a consequence is operating with less manifold vacuum. The vacuum advance mechanism retards partially, or fully, depending on the amount of throttle/vacuum. A wide open throttle will not produce any vacuum at all and the amount of ignition timing will be only what is built into the distributor as mechanical advance.

For road-going engines, vacuum advance is necessary and desirable and there is no real disadvantage in having a vacuum advance distributor on a high-performance road-going engine, provided the distributor is in good,

In practice, when the ignition timing is advanced over and above the mechanical advance by the vacuum advance, less throttle is required to maintain the same rate of speed.

Road-going engines seldom have the specifications that competition engines do (high-compression, wild cams, and so on) and are seldom subjected to the same operating conditions (constant high rpm and elevated temperatures) and, as a consequence, road-going engines are more tolerant of a vacuum advance system.

There are several reasons why vacuum advance is not required on a competition engine. Firstly, a racing engine is, strictly speaking, never under vacuum. Secondly, if the vacuum advance mechanism failed and advanced the ignition timing 10-15 degrees during a race, this would be enough to cause an engine failure through pre-ignition.

As a consequence, racing engines with distributors which have vacuum advance (and that appears to be a large number of them) should have the advance plate braized, mig welded or riveted in a permanently fixed position so that no movement is possible. The actual vacuum canister is then either removed from the distributor or left in place. Just disconnecting the vacuum advance pipe from the carburettor/inlet manifold is **not** acceptable. Movement is still possible if the advance mechanism fails. The only possible thing to do is permanently connect the movable advance plate to the base plate under it by braizing or riveting. Leave the vacuum canister in place if you want to.

A typical vacuum advance distributor on a high-performance engine. The vacuum advance mechanism's diaphragm is housed on the side of the distributor.

VACUUM ADVANCE TAKE-OFF POINT LOCATION

Between the distributor and an intake manifold/carburettor there will be a

serviceable condition. There must be no spindle wear of any consequence, the vacuum diaphragm must be in as-new condition, the location pin on the baseplate that the vacuum advance connects to and the hole in the arm of the vacuum advance must not allow any excess movement. The baseplate and the swivel plate must not have any movement other than rotary movement.

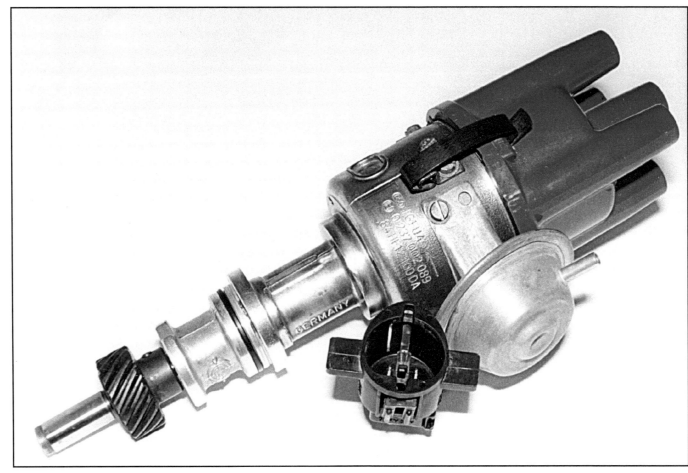

This is a Bosch distributor, with vacuum advance, as found on Ford Sierra engines.

vacuum pipe. The location of the vacuum pipe take-off point on the manifold/carburettor is important as it can affect the amount of manifold vacuum the distributor 'reads' leading to problems with non-standard carburettor/distributor pairings.

Some engines have the take-off point in the manifold or in the carburettor below the throttle butterfly which means that the distributor is designed to read full manifold vacuum. However, other engines have the vacuum take-off point immediately adjacent to the carburettor throttle butterfly which means that the distributor is designed to read only a partial amount of the full manifold vacuum.

A good example of how the vacuum take-off location can become a problem is the British-made Rover V8 engine which, when fitted with standard SUs or Strombergs, has its vacuum take-off directly adjacent to the carburettor throttle butterfly and, therefore, only partial manifold vacuum is available. However, if a Holley four-barrel carburettor and manifold is fitted to the engine, full manifold vacuum will be available (as opposed to partial vacuum).

With the standard Rover distributor/carburettor set-up, the partial manifold vacuum read by the distributor does not advance the ignition timing by more than an acceptable amount as per the design criteria. On a standard engine with the

vacuum advance disconnected, the idle speed ignition timing will be 6 degrees BTDC (as set), the total mechanical ignition timing 30 degrees BTDC, and the total ignition timing with the vacuum advance in full operation might well be approximately 40 degrees or so BTDC when cruising on a motorway. The standard ignition system is calibrated to operate like this. With the vacuum advance connected, the idle speed ignition timing might creep up to about 8 degrees BTDC which is perfectly acceptable. The moment power is demanded and the throttle opened, the vacuum reduces and the ignition timing drops back to the total mechanical ignition timing only.

A Rover V8 engine fitted with an aftermarket four barrel inlet manifold and a four barrel Holley carburettor, for instance, will have exactly the same mechanical ignition timing status, but if vacuum is taken off the inlet manifold, the vacuum advance will be on maximum at idle, which, because of the way the Lucas distributor is calibrated, means the engine could be idling with 35 degrees of ignition timing. This situation can cause real problems. Such an engine will, in fact, have a very difficult to trace misfire at idle. The car may drive alright because, when the throttle is open, no vacuum is being generated. When cruising on a motorway, however, the engine may begin misfiring and surging due to having an excessive amount of ignition timing. Having 65 degrees of ignition timing is not at all impossible.

What's happening is that the ignition timing is being over-advanced because the distributor is reading a higher vacuum than it was designed to read, and is responding appropriately to the actual amount of vacuum it is reading. What causes the misfire is that the rotor arm has been turned (advanced) so far that it is almost exactly between two distributor cap posts when the spark is delivered.

A possible solution to this problem is to limit the amount of vacuum present in the vacuum advance mechanism by building in a deliberate amount of leakage, and then restricting the bore of the connecting pipe between inlet manifold or carburettor and the vacuum canister of the distributor. A way of restricting the vacuum is to insert a short length (3in/75mm) of small diameter copper or steel pipe into the vacuum line, and then, while using a stroboscope to monitor the ignition timing, squeeze the pipe with pliers to reduce its effective crosssectional area. If this isn't enough, to further reduce the vacuum, a very small hole can be drilled in the copper or steel pipe after the restriction in the pipe (that's between the restriction pipe and the distributor) as a deliberate amount of leakage. Small drill sets are readily available for this sort of thing. Alternatively, you can start with a 0.020in hole in the copper or steel pipe and restrict the tubing between the drilled hole and the inlet manifold or carburettor. What you're doing in this case is bleeding off vacuum as a deliberate leakage factor first, and then closing the vacuum feed by squeezing the tubing. You might need to do this a couple of times before you get it right. Ensure that, one way or another, no more than 10 degrees of vacuum advance is delivered to the distributor.

It's possible with some manifold/carburettor/distributor combinations to have the opposite problem, whereby a distributor designed to read full manifold vacuum is only fed partial vacuum. The solution here would be to block the original vacuum pipe take-off on the carburettor and create a new one in the manifold so that full vacuum is read.

Caution! When any engine fitted with a vacuum advance system is being tested for acceleration, the vacuum pipe must be disconnected and the take-off point plugged. This rule applies whenever the idle and total ignition timing are being set using a strobe light.

Chapter 5

Ignition timing marks

The majority of engines have degree markings on the crankshaft pulley/ crankshaft damper rim for setting the static/idle speed ignition timing. There is no provision for setting the total ignition timing: in fact, there is virtually never any mention in manufacturers' specification listings of what the total ignition timing degrees of a given engine are. Admittedly, it's not usually necessary to know what they are because, provided the distributor is working correctly and as long as the static setting is correct, the amount the factory build into the distributor will be achieved when the total advance is 'all in.' What's not so good about not knowing what the total ignition timing degrees are and having them marked on the crankshaft pulley/ damper rim is that when the mechanical or centrifugal (call it what you want) mechanism is not working correctly there is no accurate way of checking the amount of ignition timing or lack of it.

If a strobe light is used to set the idle speed ignition timing, the

It is highly convenient to have the rim of the crankshaft damper/crankshaft pulley marked with top dead centre (TDC), the finalised idle speed and total ignition timing amounts. In this case the TDC is the straight line across the damper rim, the 18 degrees is the idle setting, and the 36-38 degrees are for the total ignition timing.

mechanical ignition timing advance can be checked to a small degree by increasing the rpm of the engine and checking to see that the damper/ pulley degree markings do actually move further on but, unfortunately, the amount of movement will not be known. **Important point!** High-performance engines need to have the total ignition timing degrees marked on to the damper so that the ignition can be accurately set to these markings rather than an accurate idle speed setting.

The crankshaft damper or crankshaft pulley will have to be marked to include increased idle speed and total ignition timing degree markings. The amount of idle speed ignition timing is not going to be more than 20 degrees while the total ignition timing is going to be anything from 32 degrees to 44 degrees depending on the particular engine. The listed combustion chamber shapes will allow the actual number of extra degree marks required to be reduced to one, or perhaps, two.

In the first instance, the new markings only need to be drawn on the damper rim/crankshaft pulley, adjacent to the fixed pointer, with a white marking pen. They can be made permanent after all of the checking and testing is finished. This way, if a mistake is made, a mark can simply be erased and a new mark drawn on to replace it. Marks are made permanent by machining, or more commonly filing, grooves, and then filling the grooves with white paint to highlight them. Permanent, accurate marks allow easy checking of the engine's total advance ignition timing using a strobe light as often as you think necessary.

CHECKING TDC MARKINGS

The timing of any engine is dependent on knowing where the true top dead center (TDC) point of the engine is. If there is error here, all other degree markings are inaccurate, but not necessarily useless if the degree of inaccuracy can be established. To avoid any confusion the TDC point must be checked. If the engine is being assembled this is a relatively easy task.

If the engine is assembled, and in the car, the procedure is a little

more complicated but TDC can still be accurately found by several means, two of which are described here.

The first method, suitable for engines with spark plug holes angled to the piston axis, involves the use of some resin core solder which is about 3mm(1/8in) in diameter. The solder is inserted through the sparkplug hole so that it will become wedged between the top of the piston crown and the cylinder head as the piston nears TDC. With the solder across the top of the piston the crankshaft is turned clockwise manually (plugs out) towards TDC. In fact, this is a dead stop method as the piston is not able to get to TDC because of the solder. The solder is soft and will not damage anything yet it will not crush unless force is applied to the crankshaft.

Once the piston contacts the solder, mark the damper/front pulley adjacent to the fixed pointer or TDC line on the block/timing cover.

Now turn the engine anti-clockwise until the piston again contacts the solder (new bit of solder, of course) stopping any further rotation of the crankshaft. Mark, with a white marking pen, the damper/crankshaft pulley adjacent to the fixed pointer or TDC line on the block/timing cover. The true TDC line on the damper/front pulley has to be exactly in the middle of the two temporary white marks, otherwise it is incorrect. Check the marks again just to be sure that a mistake has not been made.

If the manufacturer's original timing marks are incorrect, the situation will have to be remedied. Note that a pointer can be bent slightly to reposition it, while a bolted on scale can be repositioned. Alternatively, the front pulley can be moved around the crankshaft by making an offset key or the crankshaft pulley timing mark can be braised up and a new one made in the correct position. There's always something that can be done to change the positions if need be.

The second method of identifying true TDC, suitable for centrally situated sparkplugs, involves inserting a length of wood doweling down the sparkplug hole so that the bottom of the dowel rests on the top of the piston. The doweling does not have to be a neat fit into the sparkplug hole; within 1mm in diameter of the spark plug hole will be quite sufficient.

With the dowel held vertical, the crankshaft is rotated manually clockwise (plugs out) and when the TDC lines on the block and damper or front pulley are aligned, a pencil line is drawn on the doweling in line with a fixed datum point (the top of the cam cover or an engineer's rule lying across the top of a cam cover, for example).

Now rotate the engine anti-clockwise and bring the piston slowly up to TDC. When the line on the doweling draws level with the fixed datum point stop rotating the crankshaft and then check to see whether the TDC pointer/lines on the block/timing cover and damper/pulley are in alignment. If the TDC lines are in alignment, the factory markings are correct. Turn the crankshaft further and check to see that the line on the dowel does not go above the fixed datum. If the TDC marks/pointers are incorrect, they will have to be corrected using the previously described methods.

With true TDC (top dead center) marked on the damper/pulley the other marks necessary for ignition timing can be added using the following method.

MARKING CRANKSHAFT DAMPER/PULLEY

To ensure complete accuracy, the damper/pulley should be removed from the engine (it can be marked with a reasonable degree of accuracy while still on the engine). The first thing that has to be done is to measure the diameter of the damper/crankshaft pulley.

Draw a circle the diameter of the

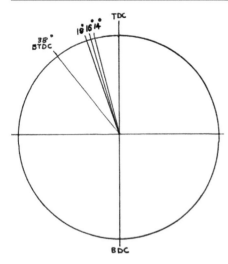

The sort of diagram you will make to show various degree markings for the crankshaft pulley/damper. By placing the pulley/damper face down on the paper the marks can be directly and very accurately transferred.

A pair of dividers set to size on the drawing and now being placed on the crankshaft pulley. One leg of the dividers is placed in the original factory machined TDC groove while the other leg is used to scribe a line on to the rim of the pulley. A white marking pen can then be used to enlarge the line so that it is suitable for strobe light use.

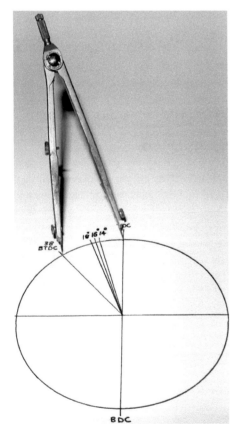

A pair of dividers being set to the correct distance as per the accurate diagram.

damper on to a piece of paper using a compass. Use a protractor to mark on the circumference of the circle the total number of ignition timing and idle speed degrees. This will give accurate dimensions which can be transferred to the damper/front pulley using engineer's dividers. This process is reasonably accurate (within 1 degree usually).

If, as will usually be the case, the idle and total ignition timing degree figures are estimates at this time, keep the piece of paper with the damper/ pulley diameter drawn on it for the final part of the degree marking procedure. Note that the final and permanent degree marking should only be carried out after the exact amounts of ignition timing have been determined by test. For the moment, the marks are of a temporary nature.

If the advance degree markings are not estimates and are known to be correct for the engine concerned, proceed with final degree marking.

PERMANENT ADVANCE DEGREE MARKING

Note that the crankshaft damper/pulley is only permanently marked after the idle speed advance test (chapter 11) and total advance test (chapter 12) have been carried out.

The damper/crankshaft pulley is removed and final markings are checked by placing the damper or crankshaft pulley face down on to the original piece of paper that the estimated advance marks were drawn on. Note that when the damper or pulley is placed face down on to the paper the markings are on the other side of the top dead centre (TDC) line that was drawn: in effect the markings are in reverse.

The estimated idle speed degree and total advance degree marks on the

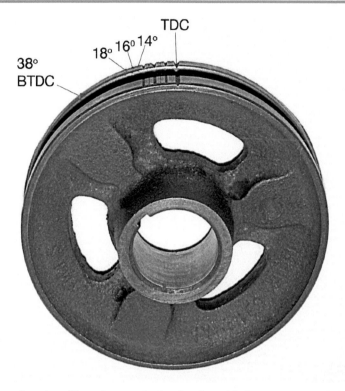

The pulley placed face down on to the drawing with the marks on the left.

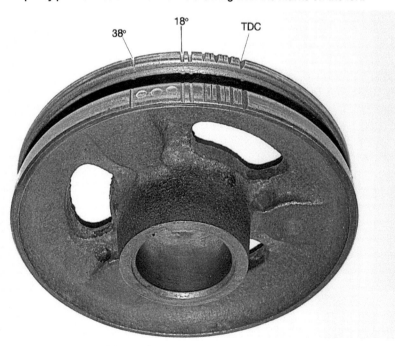

A completed marked pulley (viewed from the rear). When fitted to an engine, the marks will be opposite and similar to those shown on page 24. Most engines turn clockwise when you are facing them front on, though some don't! Always check with a workshop manual the direction of rotation of an engine.

damper/pulley will have been proven to be correct or incorrect by the tests described in chapters 11 and 12: if the temporary marks were proved to be correct, they can now be made permanent. If the testing has produced new settings, the new temporary marks should be duplicated on the paper diagram (page 34) so that the precise timing can be measured in degrees using a protractor.

Remove the pulley/damper in order to make the final permanent timing marks – it's difficult to put deep and accurate marks into the pulley/damper when it's in place. When the pulley/damper is off, it can be placed face down on the timing diagram and the optimum timing marks transferred very accurately.

The final marks should be machined into the damper/pulley square to its front face and be at least 1.0mm (0.040in) deep. This is best done using a milling machine with the damper/pulley held in a machine vice and the grooves cut using a pointed 'D bit' cutter.

An alternative method of marking is to hold the damper in a vice and use a hacksaw to cut into the rim surface. The width of a standard hacksaw blade is ideal and the depth of the cut can be limited to 1.0mm (0.040in). Care must be taken to ensure that the hacksaw cut is square to the front face of the damper/pulley; you can use a small engineer's set square.

The final optimum advance settings should be written down for future reference; things can get a bit confusing if camshaft timing marks are added to the damper/crankshaft pulleys.

Chapter 6
Distributor basics

There are certain requirements which simply must be attended to if the ignition system is going to be reliable and consistently produce the quality of spark necessary to successfully run a high-performance engine. If any of the components mentioned in the following sections is not in optimal condition, then ignition system performance will not be as good as it could be.

Mention is made of OEM (original equipment manufacturer) parts and the use of them. If the parts source available to you does not deal with OEM parts and only offers replacement parts from alternative manufacturers, use the non-original parts but check them in the manner described. The inference is not that alternative replacement parts are inferior to original equipment, it's just that original equipment parts are specifically rated for the distributor concerned. The alternative replacement may well be rated differently and therefore slightly less suitable for the specific application than the original equipment part or parts.

Irrespective of who makes the distributor parts they should all be new or near new. Fit new contact breaker points frequently in high-performance applications.

DISTRIBUTOR SPINDLE

The fit between the spindle of the distributor and the bearing in the distributor body is of vital importance if the distributor is of the contact breaker points-type. If there is any sideways movement at all (0.001in maximum clearance), the distributor has obviously been well used and is not suitable for any performance applications. This applies mainly to standard fitment points/contact sets as opposed to the more specialist Mallory distributor type points which are of excellent quality (as is reflected in their cost). Such a distributor will have to be reconditioned, which will mean that the spindle bearings and the spindle will be replaced. A less expensive option is to go to a breaker's yard and buy an identical distributor which does not have any sideways

spindle movement. This could mean that the distributor is actually off a much later engine or one with lower mileage.

The reason spindle to bearing fit is so critical is that, as the rotational speed of the spindle increases, the spindle does may not follow the central path if either it or the spindle is worn. On well worn distributors, the spindle gyrates around and the gap of the points increases, altering timing and dwell. No high-performance engine can operate efficiently with a worn distributor spindle and/or bushes.

Some distributors are notorious for wear in this area, while other distributors that fit the same engine never seem to wear. All distributors are good when new. Take the trouble to get a good distributor body with sound spindle and bushes as it is the only basis on which to build a good ignition system.

If the spindle and/or the bush(es) have any wear, have the distributor reconditioned with new parts or find an alternative distributor which is

Typical distributor drive skew gear.

A late model distributor spindle, mechanical advance mechanism, coil, rotor & stator configuration.

in excellent condition and perfectly serviceable.

DRIVE GEAR

This gear is usually driven off the camshaft and will normally not show too much sign of wear. Replace any gear with teeth that are knife-edged and look like they are worn. If in doubt about whether the gear is worn or not, check the original gear against a new one. Gears with misshapen (worn) teeth have too much backlash and timing fluctuations are a possible consequence.

ENDFLOAT/ENDPLAY

The distributor spindle's endfloat/endplay/lash is usually controlled by the amount of clearance between the drive gear and the body of the distributor. The workshop manual for your engine lists the minimum and maximum amount of endfloat permissible. If possible, set the endfloat to the minimum amount recommended by the manufacturer.

The type of washers used to control distributor spindle endfloat/lash.

CONTACT BREAKER POINTS

As a general rule, the original equipment manufacturer usually makes the best set of points for a given distributor. However, some pattern parts are just as good as OEM parts and some are better than the originals. For example, some pattern parts feature hollow contacts and a separate current conducting strap and are all-round first class components, and at a reasonable price. High-performance engines should only have the best quality points sets fitted, irrespective of the cost or manufacturer. Fit a new set of top quality points to the distributor and always carry a spare set. Note that it's inadvisable to push a metal feeler gauge through the point contacts as this can contaminate them. Place the feeler gauge next to the contacts to set the gap or use a piece of clean cardboard of the

A typical set of contact breaker points.

right thickness (micrometer measured) in place of a metal feeler gauge. Use the minimum recommended gap.

Although the world's standard engines ran on points-type distributors for about 70 (successfully), their day is over now (or it should be if you can possibly manage it). The electronic-type distributors under discussion in this book are really much the same as the earlier points-type except they don't have contact sets that wear out (giving a more reliable/better spark delivery) and also mean that a higher output coil can be used. Always check to see if there is a factory-made electronic distributor available for your engine. A very good example of points replacement with electronic means is the A-Series engine used to power the old Mini. Points were used for years (in fact, 1959 until 1982) until an electronic conversion was made for the original style of distributor. In 1985 an all new electronic distributor was made, but this new fitted the A+ A-Series engine only, which means that the early engines can't take advantage of it (not without serious modification). These later factory-made distributors are absolutely 'bullet proof.'

CONDENSER

Fit the correctly rated unit, preferably an OEM part. An under- or over-capacity condenser burns one side of the points more than the other side and a faulty condenser causes the engine to misfire. An important thing to check always is that the condenser is securely screwed to the distributor: a loose condenser will cause the engine to misfire erratically!

ELECTRONIC MODULE

The right module, correctly rated for the particular distributor, must always be fitted. Modules are frequently mounted on an aluminium plate (which acts as a heat sink) which is in turn bolted to the body (firewall/bulkhead or inner wing). Note that

A typical condenser.

there is a specific 'jelly' (dialectric grease) used to ensure that the aluminium surface of the back of an ignition module has good contact with what it's bolted to. This is to ensure correct and vital heat transfer from the module.

The electronic module requires special equipment to check its operation. If a module is suspected of being faulty (engine misfire, no spark) it has to be tested or an alternative module fitted and the engine run. Modules are usually expensive and testing the original is more practical. The module tester connects to the module and puts it through a cycle that starts at the simulated idle speed and takes it up to simulated full speed. Modules do fail, and they fail far more frequently when subjected to excessive heat and vibration. It's a good idea to carry a

A typical electronic module.

A typical rotor arm.

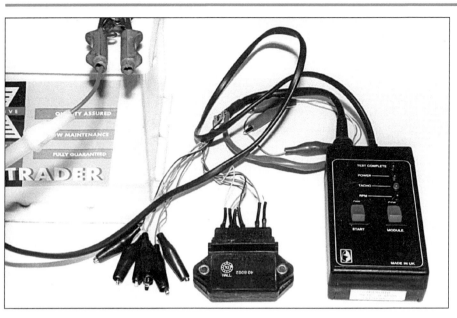

Tester light indicates pass or fail, and a miss, whether constant or intermittent, is audible.

A distributor cap which has 90 degree plug wire terminals. These caps are ideal when vertical height is limited.

A typical V8 engine distributor cap.

spare. Many garages now have excellent test equipment on site and can check modules quickly and easily.

DISTRIBUTOR CAP

Fit a new cap to the distributor and protect it from damage when it is off the distributor (when replacing points for example). Wrap the cap in a clean rag

with the leads attached and place the cap out of harm's way. Avoid scratching or knocking the cap as this can lead to cracks and a cracked cap will cause an electrical failure (engine misfire). Some manufacturers use copper contacts and some use aluminium, copper being the better of the two. Caps from Accel, Mallory and Bosch, for example, are of excellent quality and are very robust but they do cost a bit more.

ROTOR ARM

Fit a new rotor arm to the distributor. These items are relatively inexpensive

and new units are usually trouble-free. They must be a tight push fit on to the distributor spindle, it's no use having a rotor arm that flops around on the spindle. When the rotor is loose the problem can be with the spindle or the rotor arm or both. Check the fit of the rotor on to the distributor spindle and improve the fit, if necessary, by wrapping the spindle with thin tape. The tape cannot always be wrapped around the spindle for the full 360 degrees because of the spindle slot, but it can be wrapped slot edge to slot edge around the spindle.

COILS

A wide range of coils is available and some of them, while being suitable for electronic distributors, are not suitable for points-type distributors. Coils for the types of ignition systems under discussion here can be divided into four basic groups. Included in this section is a coil testing procedure with required results so that there is no doubt as to what is actually required from a coil: it also highlights the differences between various coil types.

Low voltage/'low energy' coil

The conventional coils used on all cars before the advent of electronic ignition systems in the 1980s were for use with points-type ignition systems, and on average had an output of approximately

A typical conventional standard-type coil.

17kV. They are now regarded as low voltage/'low energy' coils, and were designed to ensure both adequate points life and adequate voltage to fire the ignition. Millions of engines ran satisfactorily for years with these sorts of voltage output coils fitted to them very. However, just because they're now termed low voltage/'low energy,' in no sense does this mean 'inferior.' These coils are generally far better than they are given credit for and their replacement with an alternative 'high-performance' coil does not automatically mean more power and efficiency. There are many other things to consider – such as plug wires (low resistance type), for example – before replacing a standard type coil with an uprated coil.

The majority of points type ignition systems will run very well with this sort of coil provided the engine's compression is not too high (over 10.5:1), the rpm that the engine is turned to is not too high (up to 6500rpm) and the cylinder head/s are reasonably standard. When engines are uprated with worked heads (improved volumetric efficiency), increased compression (higher cylinder pressures) and high rpm operation, the situation changes. Having more air/fuel mixture inside the engine to compress, higher cylinder pressures and often needing more sparks per minute all add up to more coil spark being required.

High voltage/'low energy' coil

Uprated coils (Lucas Sports or Accel, for example) are available which, while still being of the same type as the previously listed coil have a higher voltage output and are rated at approximately 26 to 28kV. These coils are very similar in construction to standard coils but, because of subtle internal differences, produce more secondary voltage. These coils can be used as direct replacements for standard ignition coils and are quite satisfactory for use with all points-type ignition systems. This type of coil will not burn out the points as, while they have more voltage than the standard coils of their type, the 'energy level' of the spark they produce is not so high that it will burn the points. The 'energy level' is the same as the as the low voltage coils previously mentioned. The 'energy level,' rather than the voltage, is the vital difference between these earlier coils and the later electronic ones.

These coils are suitable for 7500 to 8000rpm operation. Once an engine has been modified (more compression, head work, camshaft, higher rpm being used) the fitting of one of these coils is recommended. Improved ignition performance (over a standard-type coil) is only possible if all other related components (plugs, points, plug wires and so on) are in perfect condition.

A typical uprated standard-type coil. This is a high voltage-type conventional construction coil that is rated at approximately 28kV, which has the same 'energy level' as a low voltage conventional coil, meaning low enough not to burn out the points prematurely.

Ballast resisted coils

When the ballast resistor is in circuit, these coils are 'low energy' coils like the two previously listed and will not burn out the points. They are typically 9 volt coils which have the 12 volts of

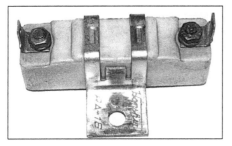

A typical ceramic-bodied ballast resistor.

A typical ballast resistor coil.

A typical oil-filled electronic coil
(up to 37kV).

Ignition coils come in all shapes and sizes.

the electrical system fed to them only for starting, during which time they are 'high energy' coils and, if run like this continuously would burn out the points. Once the ignition key is let go after the engine has started, the 12 volts of the electrical system is passed through the ballast resistor which reduces the primary voltage to the coil's rated voltage. The ballast resistor has to be correctly rated to suit the particular coil to ensure that coil has the correct voltage during normal operation. This

coil-type was a means used by car manufacturers of providing improved starting and, during starting, there's no doubt that engines equipped with this system are getting a very good spark.

Low Voltage Ballast Resistor Coil – 17kV plus (approximately) – if a ballast resistor coil is fitted to an ignition system without the ballast resistor, it is in this state a 'high energy' type coil and the points will burn out fairly quickly. The idea of putting 12 volts across a 9 volt coil to obtain a better spark is well founded, but as the points will burn out rapidly it cannot be done for very long.

High Voltage Ballast Resistor Coil 35kV (approximately) – Accel and Mallory manufacture excellent ballast resistor coils suitable for any ignition system even though these coils are primarily made for their own dual point distributors. These coils are rated at approximately 35kV and represent the best of their type. The design of these coils reduces losses, and increases the voltage as a consequence.

There is a way that 12 volts can be

put across these ballast resistor coils and an improved spark obtained when it is really needed. The method used in some racing classes, where the use of points-type ignitions is required, involves fitting a switch which is operated only when the accelerator pedal is in the full throttle position. The switch has the same function as the ignition switch during starting (bypasses the ballast resistor) and is wired in tandem with the ballast resistor. With this arrangement the points will wear out faster than normal, but nothing like as quickly as if the ballast resistor was not there at all. When the coil is getting 12 volts the spark is definitely very good and engine performance often improves because of it. All engines operating in this sort of situation need to be checked without the ballast resistor connected to see how well they go. It's then a question of making sure that the engine goes as well with the other systems rigged up.

ELECTRONIC COILS
Electronic coils are high voltage 'high energy' coils for use with electronic ignition (no contact breaker points) systems and these coils can be built to give a very high output because they do not have to take into account the erosion

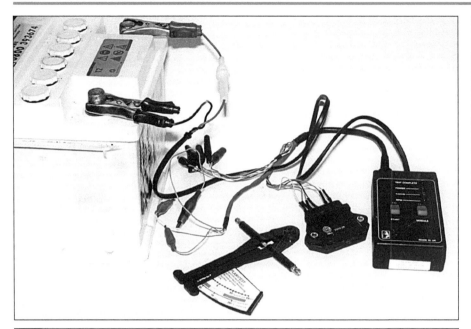

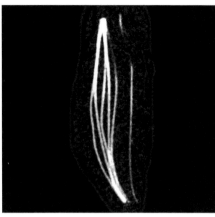

The spark of a standard 'low energy' ignition coil. Note that all of these spark photos are roughly the same scale and a reasonably true representation of the spark intensity.

Top – The equipment required to test coils.
Above – The testing rig fully set up and the arms of the Gunson Flashtest apart at the 17kV point.

of points. If this type of coil is fitted to a points-type ignition system, the points will burn out very quickly.

COIL PERFORMANCE COMPARISONS

To show the differences between the types of coils mentioned, all were tested using the type of test equipment that many workshops use. The close-up photos clearly show the differences in the size and quality of the spark.

The equipment used to test the four types of coil comprised a module/coil tester, a 12 volt battery, an ignition module, and Gunson's Flashtest.

The test equipment has a light which comes on at the start of the test cycle and another which comes on at completion of the test. The equipment makes a noise which starts from nothing and grows to a point where it sounds much the same as the artificial engine noise made by racing car games in amusement arcades. A break in the noise signifies no spark at that point.

If the spark produced by a coil is enough to constantly jump the full gap of the Gunson's Flashtest device, the coil's fine for any high-performance ignition system.

Standard coil

The first test was carried out on a standard low voltage 'low energy' coil which had a rated output of 23kV. This type of coil is typical of those fitted to the majority of engines before the advent of breakerless systems. When put through the test procedure the spark registered 17kV maximum and, if the arms of the Gunson's Flashtest were opened up, the noise emitted by the tester became intermittent, indicating that the maximum efficiency of the coil had been reached (if the arms of the Gunson's Flashtest as a standard conventional coil but their larger spark will jump a larger gap, due to the higher voltage, even though the 'energy level' is similar. These coils give five spark lines, of about the same thickness as those from standard coils which give four spark lines. This extra spark line means there is more spark

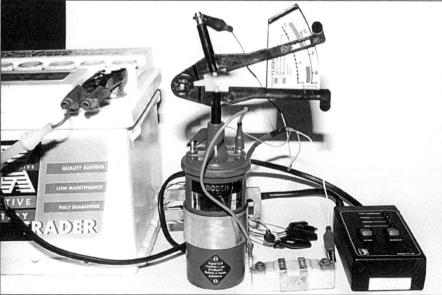

Top – A ballast resistor coil being tested without the ballast resistor in circuit. Output is the maximum (25kV) of the Gunson's Flashtest range.
Above – Same coil and same test, this time with ballast resistor in circuit (less kV produced).

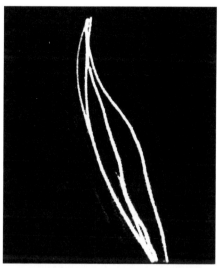

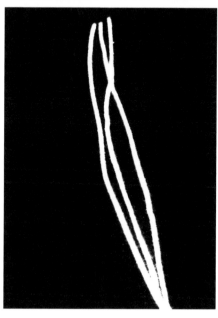

Top – The spark from a ballast resistor coil with the resistor in circuit.
Above – The spark from the same coil without the resistor in circuit.

are opened up too much, the spark will not jump the gap but this must not be allowed to happen as the module, which is part of the test apparatus, will be damaged). The number of spark lines consistently jumping the gap was five and they appeared white and very thin.

While this performance is okay to fire the plugs of a standard engine something more is needed for high-performance applications.

Sports coil

These coils are still of the same design

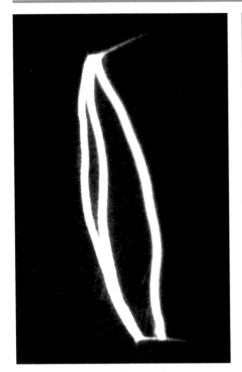

The spark produced by the electronic coil has lines which are very blue and very thick.

(25kV as opposed to 17kV from the standard coils) even though, in terms of 'energy level,' the individual spark lines are nearly identical to that of a standard coil, and the points don't burn.

Ballast resisted coils

The ballast resistor coil shows similar output to a standard coil when tested. The test is carried out with 12 volts being fed to the ballast resistor (which means 9 volts from the resistor to the 9 volt coil). With the ballast resistor in circuit, the Gunson's Flashtest showed 17kV which is the same as a standard coil.

Compared to the sports coil previously tested, there is an improvement in spark from the ballast resistor type of coil but, to get this improvement, the ballast resistor must be bypassed. With this sort of coil and the full-throttle bypass system described earlier, the engine's full throttle performance will usually be improved.

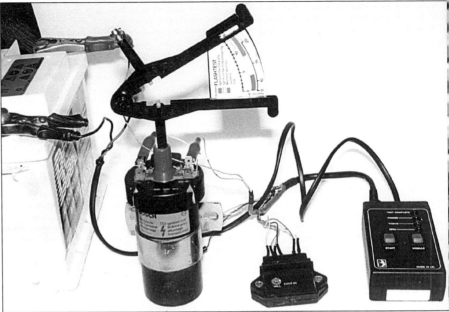

An electronic coil under test (tester arms at maximum gap).

Electronic coils

These coils are intended for use with electronic distributors and offer high voltage 'high energy' output. They should show noticeably different results on the test equipment as the spark looks very different.

Warning! these coils produce a spark that can jump 25mm (1in), or so: the very high voltage could be harmful to you, particularly if you have a pacemaker. **Caution!** – do not open the arms of the Gunson's Flashtest beyond the stop in order to see how far the spark can actually jump because the module will be damaged (power goes back).

A set of HT wires suitable for use with normal or electronic coil ignition systems.

CATEGORISING IGNITION COILS

It can be difficult to ascertain the type of coil if the particular variant's markings can't be traced back to a manufacturer for positive identification, or the labelling has come adrift. Most coils are, however, identifiable one way or another, labelled with, for instance, the name of a manufacturer, a series of letters and numbers making a code, wording such as contact points, ballast resisted or electronic only – which means the particular company's catalogue can be used to identify the coil and its designated use.

Failing that, the following Ohms-of-resistance checking procedure allows most coils to be identified, as they are generally built to basic formulas. A standard coil suitable for a points distributor, for example, will most likely have approximately 3.0Ohms of resistance, a ballast resisted coil about 1.5Ohms, and an electronic ignition coil 0.3-1.0Ohms.

Standard points-type coils generally have 350-400 turns of heavy 24-gauge copper wire on the primary winding, and about 16,000 turns of fine 45-gauge copper wire on the secondary winding. Improved output coils of this type will usually have 300-350 turns of 24-gauge wire on the primary winding, and 18,000-20,000 turns of 45-gauge wire on the secondary winding. The highest performance-rated coils of this type, such as the well-known Lucas Sports coil, have approximately 250 turns of 24-gauge wire on the primary winding, and approximately 26,000 turns of 45-gauge wire on the secondary winding, in order to obtain their 40,000 volt output. The Lucas Sports coil also had better cooling capability, via its bigger diameter case and more cooling oil.

A high energy ballast resisted coil has about 200-230 primary windings of 24-gauge wire, and 24,000 of 45-gauge wire on the secondary winding, and, if used without a 1.6Ohm ballast resistor in the circuit, would burn the points out quite quickly. With this coil arrangement, on cranking to start the engine, the battery voltage drops from 12 to about 7 or 6, perhaps even 5 as is usual when there is a 400Amp drain for example on a battery: while this is taking place, the ballast resistor is bypassed. With the ignition key in the engine-cranking position, full battery voltage, such as it is, of 5-7 volts, goes across the coil. As soon as the engine has fired, and the ignition key released and in the run position, the ballast resistor is automatically reconnected, and reducing the current to what is acceptable to make points last a suitable amount of time.

The whole principle of using a ballast resisted coil arrangement on a points ignition is purely for starting purposes, as it ensures maximum possible voltage for ignition during starting. On crank, there will usually be a maximum of 4Amp going across the points, so as not to erode them through excessive amperage in an effort to obtain a reasonable point contact service life.

High energy electronic ignition coils, on the other hand, are usually wound with fewer primary windings than all of the above, and/or more secondary windings. Some electronic coils are ballast resisted. A ballast resistor aids coil cooling, as it limits the power going to the coil – ballast resistors are operative when the ignition key is in the 'on' position, but switched off when ignition key is on crank. If, for example, the ignition key is left on for any length of time by mistake, the ballast resistor will be limiting the current going to the coil, and prevent any overheating which could lead to failure.

Constant energy electronic ignition systems have a 'power transistor,' which has a maximum current rating that must not be exceeded under starting conditions; the peak current passing through it must be what the transistor can stand, ie 4-5Amp.

There is no great heat loss in electronic coils compared to a points ignition type, as the build-up of current occurs quickly, and the coil doesn't get hot.

Constant energy in this instance means a constant 4-5Amp, irrespective of the rpm of the engine, whereas, with a points systems, the energy reduces as the rpm increases, as, when the points are closed, there is only enough time to build up to 2Amp or ¼ power. Dual points system, with their much quicker effective points closing regime, reduce this effect markedly, which is why they were used for many years in high-performance applications.

Point pitting/arcing actually occurs when the points open – current flow is positive to negative which tends to create a hole in positive and a mound on the negative. A too-low-rate capacitor won't suppress the arcing while a too-high-rate capacitor will suppress the arcing, but reduce the voltage. It's not possible to prevent this action; only to minimise the effect, through the use of matched parts.

Note that coils are made for points or electronic ignition, with it being very important to use the correct type of coil for the application. The reason for this is that the end of the secondary winding of a coil used for points ignition is connected to the positive terminal of the coil, while that of an electronic coil is connected to the negative terminal or the case – the earth to engine must not be through the power transistor, and this design measure facilitates this requirement. Using a points-type coil on an electronic ignition system may blow the power transistor, and using an electronic ignition coil with a points-type ignition results in burnt points. It is therefore advisable to match the companion coil to the distributor as per the manufacturer's recommendations.

Points and condenser

Points quality has tended to vary, and some sets have not lasted 1500-3000 miles/2500-5000km in cars. Good quality points are therefore a basic requirement, but note that many a good set of points has been prematurely burnt out due to a poor condenser – one that does not control/minimise the arcing. It used to be the norm to replace the points and condenser when the points were changed, but this was really a 'sales related' gimmick, as, in most cases, the condenser was working well and, in fact, may very often have been replaced by an inferior item. The rule is: if the points anvils wear evenly, don't replace the condenser.

To check a condenser for basic function, the end of the wire is grounded to the outer case to fully discharge it. The condenser is then 'charging' using an analogue multi-meter's own power supply, when set on Ohms of resistance by connecting the positive probe to the end of the wire, then touching the negative probe to the case/body and watching the needle movement. The needle must rise slightly from the zero position and return within about half a second. No needle movement means the condenser is defective, as it won't take a charge due to a loss of contact inside somewhere. If the needle shoots over to the right-hand side of the scale, the condenser is also defective, due to the inside shorting to the body. It is not possible to check a condenser this way with a digital multi-meter, due to the way the mechanism operates – it will not show the power surge.

Note that it isn't possible to check a condenser's basic mode of function in operation without very sophisticated measuring equipment, which is not readily available these days (a Crypton Analyser was able to measure the capacitance), so, if the points anvils wear cleanly and evenly over time and use, the condenser is a good one, and its use should be retained. As a general rule, avoid attempting to move or turn the wire in the case, as this can reduce the effectiveness of the condenser, due to a poor contact within.

While points ignitions receive much criticism these days, it has to be remembered that they were used more or less exclusively for about 75 years, magnetos being an expensive alternative; so they were not that bad, although much less reliable than modern electronic ignitions. Many classes of racing still require points-type ignition systems to be used, so, to this end, they are still in use, and therefore need to be checked and set up correctly to ensure maximum efficiency is being realised.

Coil positioning

In very cold countries, it is recommended that conventional design oil filled coils be mounted upside down so that the air-gap is at the top – on freezing, there is less chance of the coil shorting out inside. Next best position, and more usual in a more reasonable climate, is horizontal, as this means the air-gap is along the top of the body and all internal connections are immersed in oil, and the coil external terminals very accessible. Worst position is actually vertical, as the air-gap is at the top, and the connections are not 100% immersed in oil. Keeping the coil cool and away from heat sources, such as exhaust pipes, is a requirement. Coils have been known to get so hot that the oil expands sufficiently to compresses the air, push the top off, and be the cause of an engine fire due to the oil going all over the exhaust manifold and catching alight.

HIGH TENSION COIL AND SPARKPLUG WIRES

Fit new HT wires (leads) to any ignition system being used in a high-performance application. The quality of wires varies, and original equipment or standard replacement wires are all going to be of the suppression type. For road use, suppression wires are universally used to stop interference to televisions and radios. All suppression high tension wires can be tested with a meter to check their resistance. Note that even new wires can be faulty, so they should be checked, too. If a wire has too much resistance (25kOhms and above), less power will be delivered to the sparkplug and the affected cylinder could produce less power as a consequence. 3-5kOhms of resistance in an HT wire is usually enough for good suppression. The less resistance in the wire the better, provided the wire is able to offer sufficient suppression – and that's easy to check via a portable radio.

For competition use, copper core wires are still quite widely used, although this is changing now, what with the incredibly good quality suppression-type wire that is available, and the fact that many cars have to have the ignition totally shielded to avoid electro-magnetic interference. Cars with simple electrics can still use them to good effect. Copper wires are excellent conductors of electricity, and, essentially, cause no losses compared to suppression wires. Copper wires cause radio and television interference, and are not legal or suitable for use on road-going vehicles.

Checking HT wires

The following sequence of photographs shows a meter connected to HT wires. Irrespective of the manufacturer of the wires, they must all be measured for resistance on a meter, just to be sure they are okay.

In the first instance, the meter is set, via the selector dial, to read resistance (Ohms), and then set to zero, so that the readings will be as accurate as possible. The two clips are connected to each other, and then the meter is ready to be connected to an HT wire. When checking ready-made leads, a probe (use a nail) will have to be connected to one clip, so that a connection can be made to the sparkplug terminal, which is about 20mm (0.75in) down from the top of the spark plug boot or cap.

Place the clip on to the brass terminal that would normally go into the distributor cap, and hold the probe onto

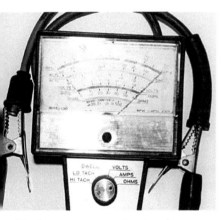

Multimeter set up to check resistance (Ohms) in an HT wire. The meter must be set to read Ohms and zeroed before the test starts.

An HT wire giving a resistance reading of 5kOhms – about the lowest you can get with suppression wires.

This new HT wire is giving a reading of 15kOhms.

This HT wire is giving a reading of 25kOhms.

The meter is reading zero resistance because this is a copper HT wire.

Maximum resistance. This wire has a break in it and is unserviceable.

the sparkplug terminal at the other end of the wire. The meter needle will move to the left if there is resistance, and the amount of resistance can be read on the meter dial.

SPARKPLUGS

In the late 1940s and early 1950s, cars used to use copper core high tension wires in conjunction with normal sparkplugs, and there was no suppression at all. If you had a radio fitted to such a car, the ignition would have to be suppressed to stop the interference. This was done by fitting special suppression caps onto the ends of the high-tension cables. By the 1960s, cars were being fitted with suppression-type high-tension wires, fitted to reduce radio and television

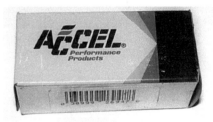

A set of contact breaker points for an aftermarket distributor. The contacts are ventilated (there's a hole through one of them) and points gap adjustment is via a screw.

An aftermarket distributor cap.

The arrangement of the contact breakers in a typical dual point distributor.

interference. However, many owners of new cars took off the suppression leads and replaced them with copper core items, for two main reasons. The first was that, visually, the spark changed from the usual yellow colour to this pale blue weak-looking spark, which couldn't even be seen in bright sunlight and which people wrongly thought was inferior. The second reason was that the new 'carbon core' suppression-type high tension wires were not very reliable when they first came out, and many failed, so people just reverted to what was known to work. The quality of the carbon core high tension wires improved over time, as did the method of connecting the terminals. Coil voltages in those days were anything from 12kV to 15kV, whereas today they're up around the 30-35kV mark. Many racing systems are up around the 60-100kV mark.

Today the use of resistor sparkplugs is nearly universal with all companies making them for road and racing use. All manner of sparkplugs are available today, from those with two and three ground electrodes with side gaps, to sparkplugs with 0.6mm diameter centre electrodes and a chamfered-end, overhead ground electrode so that the spark is unshrouded as much possible. Some sparkplugs are indexed so that they fit into the combustion chamber in a precise position so that the ground

electrode is adjacent to the roof of the combustion chamber. The three ground electrode types effectively offer tripled longevity because the spark jumps to one electrode per firing. Some ground electrodes cover only half of the centre electrode.

Conventional non-resistor sparkplugs are still available because there's still a demand for them, from the owners of older vehicles. The sparkplug companies will continue to make them because of this factor, until demand drops below the required level for economic production.

The starting point for sparkplug use is the standard original equipment items. Anything beyond road use usually requires the fitting of colder ones. Check a conversion catalogue at a motor parts dealer to find out what's available from the various manufacturers. Too hot a sparkplug can result in the engine running on when the ignition is turned off. The plug will have a very glazed appearance with a white insulator and burnt electrodes, and will result in pre-ignition, detonation and serious engine damage.

Whether a sparkplug is 'hot' or 'cold' refers to the rate of heat transfer from the sparkplug electrodes to the cylinder head. A cold sparkplug has a rapid heat transfer rate to the cylinder head, while a hot sparkplug has a slow, or slower, heat transfer rate to the cylinder head. Using too cold a sparkplug results in engine misfires, through fuel fouling, oil fouling or combustion deposits, which cause the sparkplug to be unable to fire, but never engine damage. It's better to be too cold than too hot. If you're experiencing the engine running problems mentioned here, try fitting the next 'hottest' plugs.

If anyone wants to learn how to read sparkplugs they need to buy a Champion-made sparkplug viewer which is something that is, and has been,

readily available from the Champion Sparkplug Company for years as part number CT456A and named Sparkplug Flashlight Magnifier. This tool allows a 10 times magnification viewing of the business end of a sparkplug when a sparkplug is fitted into it. What it enables you to do is view the porcelain insulator in its entirety as well as the electrodes. You can see everything you need to and make a decision as to whether you need to go colder or hotter, or leave the plug type in the engine. There isn't an engine that cannot be sorted out by this means quickly and efficiently.

Anyone involved in racing needs to always have a brand new set of sparkplugs on hand in case the engine develops a misfire during practise, or after a little bit of slow running. The ideal procedure is as follows: take the car out for a test drive and, after two laps of full bore running, change the plugs for a set of brand new ones and get going again, doing two laps to check that the engine is performing faultlessly. Once back in the pits, remove those sparkplugs, put them back in their packets, and mark them as tested. Treat them carefully and avoid dropping them (never reuse a sparkplug that has been dropped on concrete, etc, in a racing engine, as it may have been damaged inside and may fail later – like during a race!). Reinstall the old sparkplugs and continue the test drive. After all of the slow running around the pit and so on is finished, and racing proper is about to start, refit the new tested sparkplugs. Avoid slow running as this could lead to fouling and misfire.

This is a tried and tested method of always ensuring that the sparkplugs you race with are as they should be. If any slow running has to be done, take the 'race' plugs out of the engine while you're doing this. It takes a bit of extra work, of course, but it's much better to do this than run the risk of starting a race with a fouled plug or two. Some engines

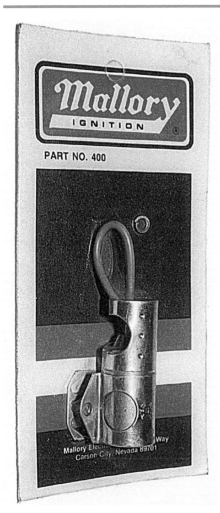

A typical aftermarket condenser.

This distributor has a single set of points and very easy to get at mechanical advance mechanism springs.

are more prone to sparkplug fouling than others (usually those with large valve guide to valve stem clearances and poor sealing, or engines that were never run-in correctly after being rebuilt).

DUAL POINT DISTRIBUTORS

These distributors are manufactured by two USA companies (Mallory and Accel) and are available for some four- and six-cylinder engines but mostly for the large range of American V8 engines. Particular mention is made of these distributors because the Mallory, for instance, comes new with a red plastic key which can be used to adjust the amount of centrifugal

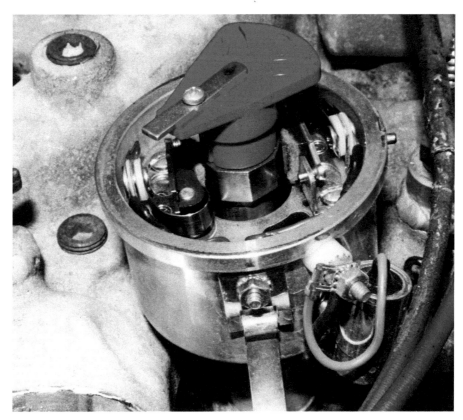

Twin points are neatly fitted into Mallory distributors. The condenser is fitted on the outside of the distributor body as there isn't any room for it inside.

This is the type of rotor arm fitted to the distributor shown previously.

advance to suit virtually any application. The rate of advance is correct for 95 per cent of applications just the way the distributor comes from the factory and the amount of advance is totally adjustable. A wide range of advance mechanism springs are available from Mallory so that alterations can be made to the rate.

Regarded by some as old technology with no possible use today, the fact remains that these distributors do give good service and good spark quality. An example of the reliability of these units is their continued use in situations where vibration and severe knocks are common (off-road racing and speedway, for instance). If there was no demand for these units, the factories concerned would have ceased producing them years ago. The parts in these distributors, and the distributors themselves, are of excellent quality. In the final analysis there isn't always a big difference in engine performance between a top quality dual points distributor and an electronic distributor, although it has to be said the electronic distributors do always tend to have better sparks because of the coils used with them. The disadvantage of the points type distributor is often the contact breaker points themselves,

or more specifically, the wear of the points' anvils. However, points wear with something like a Mallory distributor is insignificant, making them very reliable and simple ignition systems to use.

These distributors have two sets of contact breaker points, one for opening and the other for closing the circuit. On a V8, for instance, the cam lobe of the distributor is octagonal and each set of points opens and closes eight times per revolution of the distributor spindle. The positioning of the points on the baseplate is such that the first set of points opens but, just before this set of points is about to close again, the second set of points opens. Both sets of points are joined by electrical wire, when the first set of points opens nothing happens until the second set of points also opens. At this instant, when both sets of points are open at the same time, ignition occurs. Immediately after (5 degrees approximately) the second set of points opens, the first set of points closes and the circuit is closed. It's this feature of having the second set of points close the circuit very quickly

that is the main advantage of the dual point distributor. The quick closing of the circuit allows the coil the maximum time possible to build up its electrical charge.

In the single contact breaker point V8 distributor the points, after opening, have to go to full opening and then close before the circuit is closed. This takes a considerable number of degrees of distributor rotation in comparison to the dual point distributor, meaning the coil has less time to build up charge.

The early dual point distributors did not have vacuum advance units fitted to them because they were primarily intended for use on competition engines. Dual point distributors can now be bought with, or without, vacuum advance mechanisms. All street engines should have vacuum advance fitted in the interest of obtaining maximum fuel economy.

When buying either of these manufacturers' distributors only consider buying new ones or ones that have obviously had little use. Frequently these distributors get abused and to put them right can be quite costly. A new

An aftermarket distributor with vacuum advance fitted to a high-performance engine.

one comes with a guarantee and no problems of any kind are ever likely to be experienced. There are, of course, very good secondhand examples available but, unless they are virtually in as new condition, it's advisable to replace the cap, points, rotor and condenser. All parts are available for these distributors and serious users will always carry a spare cap, two sets of new points, rotor and a condenser.

AFTERMARKET ELECTRONIC DISTRIBUTORS

Electronic distributors are available from Accel and Mallory, while conversion kits are available from many other companies to convert a points-type distributor to electronic (breakerless) operation. These aftermarket distributors are of excellent quality and feature quicker advance than standard distributors: the amount of advance is also adjustable in some of them (Mallory).

Parts for both Accel and Mallory distributors, and the distributors themselves, are readily available worldwide. Note that street vehicles should have vacuum advance in the interests of obtaining maximum fuel economy, which is not always something that can be bolted on to any distributor. These two companies make distributors with or without vacuum advance mechanisms so you need to know the application before buying a distributor.

Conversion kits to give electronic ignition are available for most distributors from various manufacturers. The contact breaker points are removed and the new unit (frequently a magic eye) is bolted into the distributor using a supplementary baseplate. The rotor arm is replaced with a 'chopper' which slips on to the spindle much the same as the original rotor but note that it must be a firm push fit.

An aftermarket electronic distributor with no vacuum advance designed to be fitted into a high-performance engine, in this instance a small block Ford V8.

A distributor fitted in a very confined space on a high-performance engine. This would be impossible with the later, large cap distributor of the same type.

An aftermarket kit to convert a distributor to the electronic (breakerless) type.

The conversion module fitted to the original baseplate and the 'chopper' which provides the same function as the now redundant contact breaker points.

The Ford-made, twin-point Motorcraft distributor for the mid-1960s Hi-Performance 289ci engine had everything inside the distributor body, but no vacuum advance. Fuel economy suffered because of this. These distributors were used for racing purposes in the 1960s and 1970s.

Electronic aftermarket conversion of a distributor. Vacuum advance has been removed. This distributor is intended for racing purposes.

IGNITION FIRING AT THE SAME POINT IN EACH CYLINDER'S CYCLE

One aspect of ignition timing almost always overlooked, is that of all cylinders of the engine firing at the same number of position before top dead centre in the four-stroke cycle. In most instances, the ignition is set to the number one cylinder, and no further checking undertaken of the other cylinders' firing points. This can be a serious mistake, and cost major power loss, as it has been proven many times that it doesn't follow automatically that the other cylinders will be firing precisely at the same or within a degree of that cylinder. One degree of error between all cylinders is the minimum allowable amount. The error can be due to distributor spindle wear, and/or distributor cam wear, or, if the distributor cam is new and found to be the problem, not being made correctly in the first place, or erratic/uncontrolled centrifugal advance plate movement. It is therefore a requirement to check the accuracy of all cylinders on this basis, when an engine is being tuned after being built, to ensure that no power is lost through this means. Best estimates say less than 5 per cent of racing engines are checked.

In 1960, Lucas Industries worked closely with Formula One engine manufacturers Coventry Climax and BRM to perfect their 2SG capacitor discharge ignition systems. A part of the overall strategy was to ensure that each cylinder fired at precisely the same time as all of the others in the four-stroke cycle. To this end, a Schmitt trigger system was used, which 'picked up' the four 'pulses' per single revolution of the V8 engines from metal poles precisely positioned at 90 degrees to each other on the flywheel. This was the first application of a successful electronic type ignition system on an automotive engine.

From about 1975, car engines began to change over to electronic ignition systems, and, by about 1990, no car engine was being made which wasn't of this type; by 1995, many were crankshaft-triggered and distributor-less. This is a part of the reason why modern electronically controlled engines are so good compared to the same older, pre-electronic versions (of the very same basic engine or not), the spark intensity and the precise point of firing is absolutely identical on all cylinders. The same situation applies to carburettors versus electronic fuel-injection engines (of the same basic type or not): the right amount of fuel is injected to support combustion, as opposed to the mixture variations possible with carburettion. Electronic ignition and fuel-injection/engine management systems solved a lot of problems for the automotive industry.

Points-type distributors cam check

There is an aspect of points-type distributors that does need to be checked, to ensure that each cylinder fires at precisely the same time. While distributor cams are accurately made, they do wear, and it can mean that, while the number one cylinder is timed correctly, the others may not be, due to wear and/or faulty manufacture, or indeed by design. More than one manufacturer has made a distributor with a cam which is not perfectly symmetrical, and a cylinder or two retarded by a couple of degrees, to prevent overheating! While this measure might well increase the overall reliability, and the reduction in power not noticed in the standard environment, this is not the way to maximum efficiency with a racing engine.

This is very easy to check on a four-cylinder in-line engine, for example, provided the TDC and BDC positions, along with the total and idle speed ignition timing points, are marked on the crankshaft pulley in the two places. On all four-cylinder in-line engines, the front and rear cylinders are at TDC and BDC at the same time as are the two middle cylinders; the difference between the two pairs of cylinders is that each is 360 degrees apart in the four-stroke cycle. By clipping a strobe-timing light over each cylinder's sparkplug wire, the timing of each cylinder can to be checked individually.

A four-stroke engine requires two revolutions of the crankshaft to complete a cycle; therefore only two sets of ignition timing markings are required, as they are used twice per complete four-stroke cycle; the second set of crankshaft pulley markings can be temporary. If the firing order is 1-3-4-2, for example, the number one cylinder uses the TDC and related markings, the number three cylinder BDC and related markings, number four cylinder is then back to TDC, and number two BDC again. Each cylinder must fire at the same number of total degrees of ignition timing when the advance mechanism is fully advanced, and, if they don't, the distributor cam is at fault. This is easily checked using a strobe-light and the pick-up on each sparkplug wire in turn with the engine running. If the number one cylinder is set to 36 degrees of total ignition timing, the other three cylinders must also achieve this number.

This essential, but not so well known, checking procedure is just another in the long list that has to be made, if maximum efficiency is to be achieved.

Electronic distributors use a totally different system, which is, by design, more accurate, and not prone to the effects of any wear; although it is still a good idea to check the individual ignition timing firing points, just to be sure all is as it should be.

Chapter 7
Altering the rate of mechanical advance (part 1)

The standard type of distributor always has a mechanical advance mechanism that is controlled by two small springs. These two springs are located under the breaker plate or points plate, and on electronic distributors under the pulse generator plate. Either type of distributor (the points-type or the electronic type) will usually need to have the rate of advance changed for a high-performance application. The two original equipment springs will almost certainly be of different tension and, frequently, length. One spring (normally the strong one) will not be in tension when the distributor is at rest. This means that initially, and up until the strong spring comes under tension, one spring only is controlling the rate of advance.

For a high-performance engine the strong spring will not normally be necessary. Note that even before any testing begins the strong spring will have to be replaced with a weaker one. A good starting point is to fit another spring identical to the standard

Two typical advance springs and their attachment to anchors and the spindle plate. In this type of distributor the baseplate that carries the contact breakers needs to be removed to expose the centrifugal advance mechanism.

weaker spring. This new spring will not necessarily be the ideal spring and

another may have to be substituted if it proves not strong enough or too strong

This advance mechanism has been fitted with two weak springs in place of the normal one weak, one strong spring arrangement. The photo on the previous page has one weak spring (left) and a strong one (right). Maximum mechanical advance is reached higher up in the rpm range.

To effect very minor spring tension increases or decreases the majority of distributors have the springs connected at one end to a bendable outer post, which is very convenient when it is fitted to a distributor. Not all 'distributors have this arrangement.

On distributors where there is no adjustment via the spring post, the springs have to be changed for shorter or longer ones or the spring or springs will have to be 'tweaked' to shorten or lengthen them.

Non-standard distributor advance springs are not easy to come by so, when spring substitution is required, getting a selection of suitable' springs can be a problem. There are, fortunately, so many different types of distributor available that there are plenty of springs of different lengths and diameters to choose from and the wide choice means that there is no application requirement that cannot be covered. The only real

for the particular application. Note that it's not a good idea to remove the strong spring and start testing with only the weaker spring in place – the weak spring is never usually strong enough on its own and it could result in a too quick advance rate low down in the rpm range.

Ultimately both springs may have to be changed; certainly one spring will have to be changed to give less tension overall and, as a consequence, quicker advance.

The springs (that means both) must be under tension (however little) when they are installed in the distributor. There must not be any loose movement between the cam plate and post. Distributors set up with slack springs/ excessive movement between cam plate and post will generally advance too quickly to full advance, have erratic idle advance and a sudden jump in advance when the throttle is opened, then a slow down in the advance rate as the springs

An assortment of springs taken from a number of different distributors. Note the variations in length, diameter and wire size.

come under tension. The engine already has plenty of advance.

problem is knowing which springs to use in your particular application.

Springs can be swapped, all springs can be 'tweaked' to a certain degree to effectively lengthen or shorten them and posts can be bent in or out to a small degree. Innumerable computations are available, one way or another, to achieve the ideal rate of advance for your application.

Springs can be bought from dealers but they always want to know what pair of springs and from what engine which, of course, makes it a bit difficult as the ideal tension is not necessarily known at this point.

The best source of ignition advance springs is a breaker's yard. Huge numbers of damaged distributors, and even ones in perfect condition, get scrapped every day. Go to a breaker's yard and look for a distributor or distributors of similar diameter to that/those on the engine concerned. Remove the baseplate(s) and check to see what sizes the springs are. Expect one spring to be strong and not necessarily a tight fit on to the posts (delayed action) and the other spring to be of considerably less tension and to be under tension when installed in the distributor. Take the weak spring only and if there are several distributors available all with differing sizes (lengths and diameters) and tensions, get as big a selection as possible to improve the range of choice.

SUMMARY

At this point the stronger original advance spring will have been replaced with an alternative which is weaker by comparison and which will allow a faster rate of ignition advance for the testing of the total advance requirements. The springs will usually need to be adjusted or changed later and this is covered in Chapter 9. Some distributors don't have what can be considered a common spring size, meaning the springs used in them are much longer than most distributors. It can be difficult getting alternative springs for such distributors. In some cases suitable, coil springs will have to be made using the long tension springs that are available from engineering supply shops. The Lucas 64 DM4 electronic distributor for the A+ A-Series engine can have this problem.

Chapter 8

Altering advance mechanism to set total ignition timing

All distributors have a means of limiting the amount of advance that they can achieve. There are several ways this is done. For example, it could be by way of two slots which limit the travel by way of a pin in each slot, an arm that makes contact with a post or a post that operates between a gap cut in the side of the spindle cam plate. Irrespective of the way the advance is controlled, in every distributor there will be a way of reducing it, some will be more complicated than others to adjust.

There are several choices about when to alter the amount of mechanical advance that a distributor has.

Firstly, the idle advance and the total advance can be ascertained by test using the original distributor before it is removed from the engine to be rebuilt. Reasonable results are usually obtainable.

Secondly, the distributor can be rebuilt and an educated guess made from the information supplied on pages 17 to 20 as to what the static ignition timing might well be and on pages 21-24 for what the total ignition timing will probably be.

Thirdly, the distributor can be rebuilt without any reduction in the mechanical advance or centrifugal advance mechanism degrees, and the engine tested to measure for the static, idle speed and total ignition timing amounts required. The distributor is then partially dismantled and modified to give the exact amount of mechanical or centrifugal advance determined by test.

REDUCING TOTAL MECHANICAL ADVANCE

In the first three examples shown in the photographs on pages 57 and 58, braze would be used on the first one, as shown at the top of page 57, to build up the ends of the two curved slots mainly because it's easier to flow braze into the slots and then clean up the over-braze and size the slots. Mig welding can be used (and would be better, in fact) provided whoever is doing the work is able to put just the right amount of steel onto the ends of the slots.

The second type of stop, as shown at the bottom of page 56, would normally be Mig welded and the excess material ground off and hand filed to finished size. A Mig welded surface will last much longer than a brazed one. The use of braze on the arm, as shown in the bottom photo of page 57, would be a problem in terms of wear if the braze was the thickness of the steel plate. However, if the amount of braze placed on the arm is about $1/4$in/6mm in height, the wear issue will be reduced to a minimum.

The third type is the slot arrangement, shown at the top of page 58. This one can be either brazed or Mig welded. The use of braze on the cutout slot of the third distributor on page 58 isn't a problem in terms of wear as the Hypalon sleeve is in-between, and there's no metal-to-metal contact. Most people Mig weld these.

The fourth type of advance limiting arrangement, shown in the lower photo

With this type of advance governing mechanism, reducing the length of the slots reduces total advance.

With this type of advance governing mechanism, where a stop in the arm contacts a spring post, adding material to the stop on the arm reduces total advance.

on page 58, requires that a small, high-tensile steel sleeve be made and pressed over the original pin. It's then silver-soldered or brazed to the original pin to reduce any possibility of movement in service.

Braze is most often used for the first example although it will wear over time and cause the amount of mechanical advance to increase. The rate of wear is slow provided the two slot lengths are the same and both limiting the travel of the two pins equally. Care and accurate filing are needed to get this arrangement right. Braze is used a lot for this sort of thing because, even though it's softer than the original components, it's comparative softness to Mig weld, for example, means that your modification work can be cleaned up reasonably easily and neatly.

An alternative to brazing is to use a hard surfacing agent such as a 'Stellite' which is put on with a brazing torch and is as hard if not harder than the original components. The disadvantage is that, if more material than necessary is put on,

With this type of advance governing mechanism, adding material to the stop or the arm reduces the total amount of advance. In this case you would reduce the slot length because of the Hypalon sleeve which fits over the post. The black Hypalon sleeve is fitted to this distributor.

With this pin and hole type of advance governing mechanism, adding material to the pin (by way of a sleeve) reduces total advance.

it is very difficult to remove the excess neatly. If the component being built up with 'Stellite' is easy to get at, this is an excellent way of building the part up. Anyone proficient in using a brazing torch and using 'Stellite' (or any similar material) will be able to carry out the procedure quite easily.

If the distributor rotates clockwise the left-hand edge of the slot or cut-out in the cam plate is brazed up and, conversely, if the distributor rotates anti-clockwise the right hand edge of the cam plate is brazed to build it up. The edge that the springs pull the cam plate against when the engine is stationary is the edge that needs to be built up. The reason it is done on this side is to advance the cam plate and, as a consequence, put slightly more tension on the springs. The end of the arm as shown in the top photo on this page is built up if the distributor rotates clockwise.

Whatever method of controlling the total amount of advance used by the distributor manufacturer, it can all

Distributor partially stripped to reveal advance mechanism and advance springs removed. The actual amount of advance delivered by the centrifugal mechanism can now be measured.

Modelling clay/Plasticine used to immobilise the distributor spindle.

be reduced one way or another. The examples shown here are the more common ones.

Most distributors for high-performance applications need the total amount of mechanical ignition timing advance to be reduced from the usual built-in 12 to 17 distributor degrees to between 8-10 distributor degrees (multiply these figures by 2 to get crankshaft degrees). The crankshaft rotates twice to the camshaft's once and ignition timing degrees are always quoted in crankshaft degrees for convenience of measuring them via a means easy to see on the engine.

How much to limit advance

In the first instance, the distributor has to be checked to find out how many degrees of ignition timing advance have been built into the distributor by the original manufacturer, assuming it is standard, or how many degrees of ignition timing advance are in the

distributor now. The simplest way of doing this is to partially dismantle the distributor, which involves removing the points plate or pulse generator plate and both advance springs. Removing the advance springs allows the mechanical advance mechanism to be moved easily from the static position to the full advance position. This would not be possible if the springs were left in the distributor.

With the distributor body prepared like this the spindle has to be locked in a position to prevent it rotating. The means of locking the distributor spindle can be as simple as using modelling clay/Plasticine moulded on to the body of the distributor and the spindle drive gear or drive plate.

Next, a pointer is cut out of sheet aluminium or tin plate or any other suitable material. The pointer has to be long enough to go right to the edge or maximum diameter of the distributor body. With the spindle locked in position the pointer is fixed to the top of the spindle. A line can be scribed on to the body of the distributor, or the pointer lined up with a corner or edge which will act as a datum point to measure from.

Pointer fixed to the top of the distributor spindle with modelling clay/Plasticine.

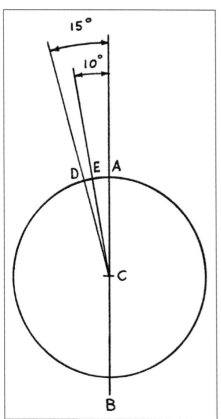

A circle of the same diameter as the distributor body with lines indicating degrees of advance and identifying letters.

Side view of the distributor body showing pointer, area painted with light coloured paint and scribed line indicating the static advance position.

With the main distributor spindle locked, the pointer fitted to the top of the cam plate and the cam plate in the static position, the side of the distributor is marked with a white marking pen and a line scribed adjacent to the pointer. The distributor is now in the zero position.

With the distributor set in this position use a small screwdriver to move the mechanical advance mechanism the correct way (advance) from the static position to the full advance position. The pointer affixed to the top of the main distributor spindle will rotate either clockwise or anti-clockwise depending on the direction of rotation. With the mechanism in the full advance position, scribe a line on to the side of the distributor body adjacent to the pointer.

The side of the distributor now has two scribed lines on it. One mark is the static advance point and the other is the full advance point. These two scribed lines represent the total amount of travel of the mechanical advance built into the individual distributor. Use the screwdriver to move the advance mechanism back to the static position. The pointer must line up with the first scribed line. If it

Move the centrifugal advance mechanism to its stops and mark the distributor body as shown.

paper. Firstly a circle of appropriate diameter (64.5mm/2.540in in our example) is drawn on to a piece of paper. A line is drawn through the centre (marked 'C') of the circle and on past the circumference of the circle (marked 'AB'). Dividers are then set to the distance between the two scribed lines (8.0mm/0.315in in our example) and this distance transferred on to the circumference of the circle starting from where the line intersects the circumference at 'A' and across to 'D.' A line is drawn on the paper from 'C' to 'D' and then a protractor is used to measure the angle formed between points 'A,' 'C' and 'D.'

In our example, the amount of advance is 15 degrees at the distributor (30 degrees at the crankshaft). If, for example, the total centrifugal/mechanical advance is to be reduced to 10 degrees at the distributor (20

Measure the diameter of the distributor body using a vernier caliper.

does the spindle has remained stationary during the test. Repeat the procedure and check the settings.

The distance between the two scribed lines is now measured as accurately as possible with a vernier caliper. In our example the distance between the two lines is 8.0mm (0.315in). The next step is to measure the diameter of the distributor body and in our example it measures 64.5mm (2.540in) in diameter. This is enough information to work out how much mechanical advance the distributor has. It is not perfectly accurate but it is accurate enough. Further to this, the distributor body's diameter is measured where the scribed lines have been placed. This is to assist with the next part of the operation of transposing the scribed lines onto paper.

This information is now put on

Measure the distance between the static and full advance point marks with a vernier caliper.

degrees at the crankshaft), draw a further line on the diagram for 10 degrees which will become 'C' to 'E.' Using a vernier, measure the distance between 'A' and 'E' on the circumference of the circle. In our example that distance is 5.5mm (0.215in). This dimension is then transferred to the side of the distributor with the vernier caliper.

On the side of the distributor there will now be three lines. The distributor is reset with the pointer lined up with the middle line, the point which is now going to be the full advance position. With the pointer in this position, it's short of the full travel by 2.5mm (0.097in). Further to this there will now be a gap between the pin and the end of the advance slot in the cam plate. It's this gap which must now be measured because the slot must be reduced by this amount to restrict advance to the required amount.

An easy way to measure the size of the gap is to use a small drill bit. You can use as a gauge anything round that will fit into the exact gap and then measure the gauge with a vernier caliper or a micrometer to ascertain the size of the gap. The gap in our example distributor measured 0.9mm (0.036in).

No claim is made that this method of measuring the advance degrees is absolutely perfect, but it's usually quite satisfactory and, in the final analysis, all final degree measuring is checked using a strobe light and an accurately marked crankshaft damper/front pulley. So, if an error is made in the measuring, it can be checked and, if found to be inaccurate, the work rectified. One way or another the reworked distributor can be engineered to an accuracy of 1 degree.

At worst the modified gap can be too small or too large. If the gap is too small material can be removed from the stop and if the gap is too large more braze or Mig weld can be applied to correct the problem.

One thing that is important is that the posts hit their respective stops at the same time, or within 0.1mm (0.004in) of each other (if there are two posts).

WHAT HAPPENS IF THE DISTRIBUTOR IS NOT MODIFIED?

Most standard engines only have a few degrees of static and idle speed ignition timing, such as 2-8 degrees BTDC (before top dead centre) – while a high-performance engine will start best with between 10-16 degrees BTDC of static ignition timing and idle best with between 12-20 degrees of ignition timing.

The pointer aligned with the middle line which indicates the required amount of maximum mechanical advance.

If a standard distributor which has a lot of mechanical or centrifugal advance was set at 12-14 degrees BTDC static ignition timing, for example, runs extremely well like this, the total ignition timing could be anything from 40-46 degrees BTDC. This amount of total ignition timing is not acceptable.

Sure, it's possible to just leave the static advance at the standard setting or, perhaps, advance it a couple of degrees and time the engine so that the total amount of ignition timing is right (or even slightly over-advanced by a couple of degrees) for the production of full power. This, in fact, is the usual scenario but a distributor that has a lot of built-in mechanical or centrifugal advance cannot usually give ideal static, idle speed and total ignition timing. The whole objective of modifying the distributor in the described manner is to have optimum ignition timing in all engine loading and rpm situations.

Engines that are set-up with the

correct amount of total ignition timing but insufficient static and idle advance sound terrible at low rpm. They sound 'flat' and often 'spit back' through the induction system, the engine does not accelerate cleanly and if the engine is in a car it is virtually undriveable unless high rpm such as 3000-4000rpm is used and then they 'come alive.' These problems can be avoided if the ignition is modified correctly to suit the engine's application and state of tune.

It's worth noting that performance engines which have had more static and/or idle speed ignition timing and less mechanical or centrifugal advance than the standard production engines is nothing new. An example of this is the Lucas distributor used in production four cylinder Fords in the 1960s. When Ford produced the Lotus Cortina engine Lucas supplied a distributor that did not have vacuum advance and which had approximately 10 degrees of advance built into the distributor, which is 20 degrees of ignition timing as measured on the crankshaft with a strobe light. This particular distributor was fitted, by enthusiasts and engine builders, to all manner of small Ford racing engines at that time because its timing was basically correct just as it came. The static advance could be set, for example, at 16 degrees BTDC and the total advance was still only 36 BTDC. So, some production distributors do, in fact, have the right amount of centrifugal or mechanical advance built into them and setting the static ignition timing to more than standard will see the total ignition timing set correctly as well. It must be accepted, though, that for high-performance applications most original equipment distributors do have to be modified to reduce the amount of built-in mechanical advance.

Chapter 9
Altering the rate of mechanical advance (part 2)

ESTABLISHING RATE OF ADVANCE

As the idle speed and the total ignition timing figures are now known, the rate of advance can now be measured and adjusted as necessary. The engine must be set at an idle speed that is conducive to smooth running.

An example would be an engine idling at 1250rpm which has 18 degrees BTDC of idle speed ignition timing a total amount of ignition timing of 34 degrees.

To make it easier to see the rate of advance, mark the damper or pulley between the 18 degree mark and the 34 degree mark with three reasonably equally spaced large dots using a white marking pen. A graph can be drawn up later which will show, after the test, how the engine's ignition timing advances and when it reaches the total ignition advance point. Note down the amounts of ignition timing degrees at 1000rpm, 1500rpm, 2000rpm, 2500rpm and so on until the ignition timing stops advancing. Assistance is required to do this test; the

Rim of pulley marked with three white dots between the 18 and 34 degree marks. There are near enough 4 degrees between the dot centres.

assistant must hold the rpm steady while watching a tachometer (rev counter) so that an accurate assessment of the number of ignition timing degrees at given engine speeds can be made.

With strobe light connected, raise the engine rpm from idle speed to 1500rpm and, hold it there, note the ignition timing degrees, and repeat at 2000rpm and 2500rpm. The strobe

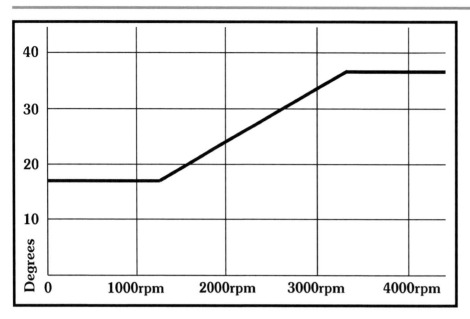

Graph shows desirable advance rate between 18 and 38 degrees BTDC.

light will flash and put enough light on to the crankshaft damper/pulley for a comparison to be made of where the TDC mark was originally at idle and where it has moved to in relation to the temporary dots. Repeat this process at 2750rpm, which is the earliest the ignition timing should ever be fully mechanically advanced on any engine, and then try 3000rpm, 3250rpm, 3500rpm, and 3750rpm. You may have to go as high as 4000rpm to get the mechanical advance to stop advancing and, in a few cases, perhaps 5000rpm on engines fitted with very long duration camshafts that don't develop maximum torque until this amount of rpm, or engines with too much compression for the octane rating of the fuel being used in them.

The next stage is to ensure that the ignition timing is 'all in,' or fully advanced, before the rpm that produces maximum torque without any signs of 'pinking.' It's a delicate balance. The objective of the exercise is to have sufficient ignition timing present, but no more than necessary, caused the engine to develop the highest amount of torque

it is capable of over as wide an rpm band as possible. There's no point having an engine that is capable of developing its best torque between 4000 and 5000rpm with the ignition timing still advancing and getting to the optimum amount at 4500rpm. The ignition timing needs to be 'all in' at least at the start of the maximum torque plateau which, in the example, is 4000rpm. What is usual in such a case is to have the ignition timing fully advanced at 3750rpm. However, few engines can tolerate their ignition timing being 'all in' or fully advanced at 2500rpm, but quite a few can tolerate it at 2750rpm. It isn't actually worth having the ignition timing 'all in' or fully advanced before this amount of rpm, so consider 2750rpm to be the earliest possible for **any** engine.

The accompanying graph shows the ignition timing starting to increase at approximately 1300rpm and being fully advanced at approximately 3300rpm. If this is too slow a rate, change one of the springs for one which is weaker but which is of equal fitted tension when fitted to the advance plate/'cam plate.' This will cause the ignition timing to start

advancing at the same point (1300rpm) but then advance quicker as the rpm rises. There is quite a lot you can do here to end up with the perfect rate of ignition timing advance. This is where having a very good range of ignition advance springs comes in.

ALTERING THE RATE OF ADVANCE

If the ignition timing advances too quickly, such as the ignition timing being 'all in' or totally advanced at say 2200-2400rpm, expect the engine to exhibit mechanical harshness and not accelerate from the idle rpm quickly or cleanly. This fast advance rate is no good at all; it's just too quick, and can cause mechanical damage to an engine.

Note that it's usually the older style pushrod-operated and single overhead camshaft two valve per cylinder engines that develop maximum power at no more than 7000rpm that 'like' the ignition timing to be 'all in' or fully advanced around 2750-3250rpm. These engines always tend to develop maximum torque irrespective of what duration camshaft is fitted to them, in the rpm range of 3000-5000rpm. The more modern four valve per cylinder engines tend to follow suit on the basis of the production of torque, except they do not reach their maximum air-flow capability and, therefore, point of maximum power, at 7000rpm but much higher, at 8000-9000rpm or more.

It's quite possible to have an engine's ignition timing advancing too quickly and to lose a lot of acceleration because of it. So, while the idle speed ignition timing and the total amount of mechanical ignition timing can both have been quite accurately arrived at by test, unless the rate of advance is checked and optimised to suit the particular engine, the overall performance potential of the engine will be considerably reduced as a consequence.

To be on the safe side, the advance

springs should provide enough tension to ensure that the engine does not advance to the full amount before 2750rpm. Admittedly, the engine will have to be tested to find out what the existing rate of advance is, but as this test is conducted with the vehicle stationary the engine is not under load. It is exceedingly unlikely (near impossible) that you would damage a free revving (no load) engine as a consequence of momentarily running it with too rapid a rate of ignition timing advance.

The vast majority of production type engines will require their ignition timings to be 'all in' or fully advanced between 2750rpm to 3750rpm. 'Start high and come down slowly' is a well founded principle here. Go down to 2750rpm if, through thorough testing, you find there is no 'pinking,' engine harshness, or worse, detonation, because the ignition timing is being advanced too quickly.

Once you are fairly happy with the advance rate of the engine running without load, as determined during stationary testing, the engine should be tested again under load conditions. If the engine is in a car this will involve road or track testing.

The object of the exercise now becomes one of checking the rate of acceleration with the combination of advance springs fitted into the distributor. The rate of ignition timing advance that ultimately causes the engine to accelerate the best is the optimum rate. This is the acid test, and is the one that really matters.

If the engine is in a road-going car it must not 'pink' under acceleration with wide open throttle from a standing start, no matter whether it is an automatic shift or a manual shift. Most manual shift cars can be made to 'pink' if the engine is forced to 'lug' in high gear at an unreasonably low rpm. 'Pinking' induced by this sort of treatment can be disregarded because no car enthusiast with a modified engine would ever consider doing this for long, only momentarily before they changed to a lower gear.

Both advance springs, or one spring only, can be changed for slightly stronger springs, shortened or the posts tweaked to effect an increase in spring tension if the engine 'pinks' under load. Conversely, spring tension can be reduced if there is no sign of 'pinking' under full acceleration. Weaker springs, or one weaker spring, can be fitted to effect this reduction.

The ignition timing needs to be advanced at the quickest rate which precludes 'pinking.'

For the majority of high-performance engines full advance will likely need to be achieved between 3000-3500rpm. This can be expanded to give a maximum of 3750 down to a minimum of 2750rpm. In most applications 4000-4250rpm, for example, will be much too high in the rpm range. You might consider doing this, however, for a very high compression engine which uses an octane rating of fuel that is not quite high enough. Putting off achieving full advance may mean that the engine has slightly less ignition timing advance at maximum torque but, as the rpm increases past this point, the ignition timing advances a little bit more and better engine performance is often achieved.

If an engine 'pinks' and continues to do so at engine speeds over the known full advance rpm, but the 'pinking' ceases as the engine speed approaches maximum rpm, the chances are that the engine has slightly too much compression for the octane rating of the fuel used. This can be checked quite easily by draining the fuel tank and refilling with a higher RON and MON octane fuel. If the engine then stops 'pinking' and develops more power, or has more 'go' in it, the engine definitely has too much compression. Retarding the timing by whatever means is technically the wrong way to fix this sort of problem. The compression ratio really needs to be reduced or higher RON and MON octane fuel used all of the time. Engine damage will probably result if gross 'pinking' is allowed to continue.

If the engine is in a car which will be used only on the track, the engine should be tested under full acceleration through the gears from a standing start and at no time is any 'pinking' permissible. Further to this, when the car is being driven around the pits or at low rpm the engine should not be 'fussy,' nor should it require huge amounts of throttle to get the car moving.

The objective of modifying any distributor is to end up with an engine that is as tractable as possible throughout the rpm range, irrespective of the state of tune (specification-wise) of the particular engine.

Chapter 10
Checking the quality of the spark

With all new parts fitted and the engine up and running, certain checks are made to ensure that, overall, the ignition system is functioning correctly. Ultimately, what matters is how much power is delivered to the sparkplug and that the sparkplugs are firing correctly.

A great many engines never produce their optimum response and top end power because the amount of spark at the sparkplug electrode on ignition is NOT correct. This statement is not as far-fetched as it may seem. NO engine, of a performance type or not, will produce a good and satisfactory power output if the amount of spark jumping the gap of the sparkplug is low. Just because an engine starts, runs, turns high rpm and doesn't misfire under load doesn't mean that it's right; it has to be proven to be right and that means the components tested to see that they meet the required standard. To fire a high compression engine, especially 10.0:1 and above, the condition of the electrical system has to be perfect before any testing

can be carried out, kV at the sparkplug must be known. The correctness of the electrical circuitry in general, and the ignition circuitry in particular cannot be emphasised enough. There can be no short cuts here.

WIRING AND CONNECTIONS

Fit brand new wires and new connectors wherever possible to the entire ignition system. Where wires are difficult to renew, such as in an existing wiring loom, if possible remove the old connectors, cut back the wire to expose a new clean copper core and put new connectors on. All terminals (ignition switch terminals, coil terminals, and so on) must be absolutely clean with no corrosion present. Breaks in wires, corroded and/or loose terminals can be the cause of a reduction in voltage or an intermittent electrical fault. It's often better to rewire the entire ignition circuit, if not the whole car, if there's anything suspect about the wiring.

ALTERNATOR

All engines (road-going or competition) should be fitted with a good alternator. Road-going vehicles, for instance, have to have a good charging system to continue running, and the voltage measured across the battery terminals, while the engine is running and charging, should be 13.2-14.2 volts. An alternator which is putting out this amount of voltage is what is required, not one that is putting out just 12.2-12.4 volts at maximum rpm.

The practice of using a large capacity 12 volt battery instead of a generator for a competition engine is just **not** acceptable. The ignition system will have insufficient voltage and, although the engine will run, and run quite well, it will not run as well as when the voltage available is up to 13.2-14.2 across the battery terminals (note that a good battery holds 12.3-12.5 volts and not 12 volts when fully charged).

Fit a new or rebuilt alternator to the engine and check that the voltage output is as it should be; do not simply put a new alternator on to an engine and assume that the voltage output is correct. Check it and note the voltage across the battery with the engine running: check the output of the alternator whenever ignition troubles are experienced and see that the figures still match those originally recorded.

Alternators come in varying sizes and weights and, as lightness is a prerequisite for all racing engines, the smallest and lightest are usually sought for this purpose. Small, lightweight, high output alternators are fitted to many small car engines these days, yet they are 35-45 amp output ones. All alternators can be slowed down by changing the diameter of their pulleys for larger custom made aluminium ones. It's very often acceptable to slow an alternator down to crankshaft speed. Most alternators are putting out voltage at 800-900rpm (alternator rpm that is). The alternator must be putting out 13.2-14.2 volts throughout the engine rpm range.

IGNITION SWITCH

A new ignition key/switch should always be included as a part of the ignition system because, if the ignition switch fails, it will not send 12 volts consistently to the primary side of the coil and this will show up as a very weak spark (low kV at the plug). Problems that often stem from the ignition switch (loose contacts) include intermittent faults such as an engine misfire, hard starting (sometimes), no ignition (sometimes) and, eventually, no ignition at all.

Fit the best quality switch available, and keep in mind that ignition switches are not noted for their ability to tolerate a lot of vibration. The mechanism inside the switch becomes loose and ends up making poor contact or no contact.

Check with a volt meter that there is 12 volts going to the primary ('+') side

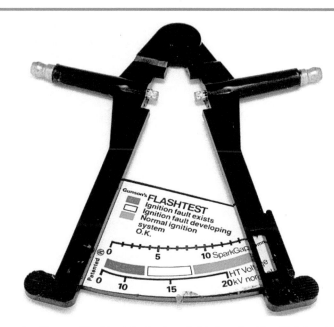

The inexpensive Gunson Flashtest device is suitable for checking high tension voltage on a contact breaker-type ignition system or an electronic one.

Gunson Flashtest being used to check voltage at the sparkplug cap end of an **HT** wire.

of the coil. Note that marine use ignition switches tend to be more robust than automotive ones.

CHECK HIGH TENSION CURRENT

A simple tool that can check the kV going to the sparkplugs is the Gunson Flashtest. This is an inexpensive tool made of plastic with a direct reading scale. The scale is proportional to the size of the gap and the gap, which the spark must jump, is increased or decreased by opening and closing the arms of the device.

Caution! The Gunson Flashtest can

be used on either a points-type ignition system or an electronic ignition but you must not open the Flashtest out beyond the stop and check the module to see exactly how big a gap the particular module can make a spark jump. If you do this, a perfectly good module will be irreparably damaged.

The kV available to the sparkplug is read directly off the Flashtest scale. If the kV is in the green part of the scale the ignition is okay, if the kV is in the white or red part of the scale there is something wrong.

To check the high tension (HT) sparkplug wires take the wire off a sparkplug (one at a time) and connect it to a terminal of the gauge, earth the other end of the gauge to the engine. Turn the engine over (sparkplugs out) and see what kV is present. What you will know if the gauge is in the green is that all parts of the ignition system before the end of the plug wire are in good order and the spark is sufficient. This, of course, does not mean that the sparkplugs themselves are okay. Note the kV reading of each plug lead.

A more sophisticated meter is the Snap-on Tools MT 2700 DIS/kV probe. This slide back volt meter can be used to test any ignition system, even when the engine is being run up on rolling road or engine dyno. It's an ideal bit of kit for doing this because readings are being taken when the engine is under maximum loading. The meter uses an inductive pick-up which lightly slips over the ignition lead (or coil lead) and the dial on the meter is turned until the light stays on and is then turned the other way until the light starts to flicker. A reading is then taken. This meter does not give a true kV reading, but it does not matter that it doesn't. Essentially a reading of 2-3kV means that there is a fault, while 8-12kV in the ignition wire means the system is working correctly. 20kV means that there is definitely something wrong. The coil

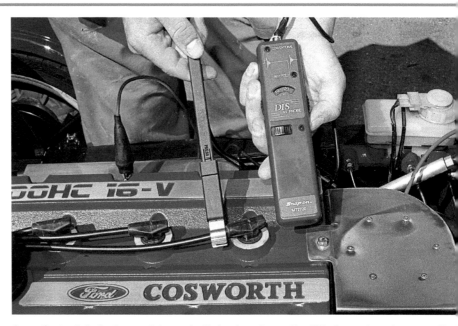

Snap-On tools inductance pick-up. A clip is placed over the HT wire and a voltage reading is indicated on the instrument's scale.

HT wire will have readings of 10-16kV for a system that is working correctly, while 3kV means that something is wrong. 20kV-plus also means that something is wrong. Certainly the integrity of the spark can be checked with this equipment and faults easily diagnosed.

These types of meter will pick up the fact that the sparkplug is faulty. If the engine is missing, for instance, all of the sparkplug wires are checked for kV. A lead that gives a low reading should have the sparkplug changed and a further reading taken after the change. If the plug was at fault the reading will rise to match, approximately, that of the other leads. Alternatively, if a low reading is found and the sparkplug is difficult to get at, change the HT wire for a new one (resistance tested) and check the kV in the new lead. If the reading rises to match approximately the others the lead was at fault. If the reading stays the same the plug is at fault and will have to be replaced.

The output of the coil can be checked by slipping the inductance pick-up over the coil lead and taking a

reading. The reading will frequently be the same as the plug lead reading or slightly above (2kV).

An alternative is to have the engine checked at an auto-electrical specialist which will use a sophisticated analyzer. This way all doubt will be removed as to the integrity of the spark. The cost for checking the engine will be reasonable and if there is anything wrong it will be quickly found.

One point about the electrical testing described so far is that it has all been carried out without the engine being under load conditions, and an engine under load does not necessarily perform in the same way. The fact that electricity takes the path of least resistance always applies so what was regarded as a completely satisfactory performance in unloaded condition can suddenly become a quite unsatisfactory performance under load. When this happens all of the ignition system components, new or used, must be checked for faults.

Rolling road operators have scientific diagnostic equipment to check the voltage output, and this should be done just to make sure that all cylinders are receiving a suitable voltage when the engine is under load. **Caution!** - Be mindful of the fact that an engine will run with a low kV going to the sparkplugs, so even though the engine starts easy and basically sounds quite good, it's quite vital to know exactly what the

kV is that is that is igniting the air/fuel mixture. Always aim for the highest kV possible from the type of coil being used as opposed to the low or mid side of the tolerance, as it really does make a difference to how an engine will go. This aspect of the ignition system has caught a lot of people out over the years, and been the cause of a lot of slow engines.

High-performance engines are often not the same as standard road going engines here, and magnify problems. The appropriate values must be realised, and on a high-performance engine those values need to be on the high side of the known tolerances!

Chapter 11
Establishing the correct idle advance

By this stage the distributor will have been fitted with ignition advance springs which, combined, have less tension than the standard originals at full advance. As a result the mechanical advance is going to be quicker to the fully advanced point than it was when standard, but it may still not be quick enough or, conversely, may be too quick. In most instances, both of the mechanical advance springs will be under tension when fitted to the distributor cam-plate so that the amount of advance built into the distributor will be all that's in operation at idle speed. The exception to this is when the static ignition timing is going to be quite low so that the starter motor is able to turn over the engine easily, yet the engine requires a higher amount of idle speed ignition timing to obtain optimum smooth idle characteristics. In such cases one spring is usually a loose fit over the posts while the other is in tension.

Fit the distributor to the engine and time it, as near as possible to 8-10 degrees BTDC. This is quite easy with a points-type ignition system as the crankshaft damper/front pulley can be positioned using the appropriate marks and the distributor rotated until the points just open. The setting will be accurate enough to start the engine. Electronic distributors have the trigger lined up with the stator posts at the 8-10 degree mark BTDC on the crankshaft, which will usually prove to be about right for starting purposes. The engine can then be started and warmed up.

Provided the engine is idling at the approximate rpm recommended for the camshaft, the testing can begin. If the engine has carburetor problems, for example, meaningful testing will prove difficult. Resetting an ignition system in the manner described here is not a cure-all for induction problems so the following testing technique assumes that the engine is running well overall.

Put a strobe light on the engine to see where the ignition timing actually is at idle. If it isn't at 8 degrees BTDC set it there now, and then set the idle speed to that recommended for the duration listing of the camshaft fitted into the engine. With the engine idling smoothly, loosen the distributor and advance the ignition timing to 10 degrees BTDC and note if there is an improvement in the smoothness of the engine idle and whether the rpm increases. If the idle speed increased or the smoothness improves, the engine has responded to the increased ignition timing. Advance the ignition timing in 2 degree increments until 16 degrees of idle speed ignition timing is reached, noting what happens each time you do so. You might well have to slow the idle speed down each time the ignition timing is advanced to keep the engine speed down to the required amount. The object of the exercise is to find the amount of ignition timing that causes the smoothest even idle at the applicable idle rpm, as well as easy starting.

Note that the idle speed needs to be kept as slow as reasonable for the duration of the camshaft fitted into the engine, but obviously it has to be fast enough so as not to cause engine acceleration pickup problems. The idle figures listed on page 13 are about right for most engines. If your engine idles too fast, you might end up with 'running on' or gear engagement problems. The optimum idle speed can be found for any engine with a bit of patience and, once found, it won't change until the specification of the engine is changed.

All engines seem to have an ideal idle speed which isn't too fast and isn't too slow and it's up to whoever is tuning the engine to find that 'right' idle speed. Once found the engine is always set to it. Tuning engines is really a case of experimentation to find the optimum settings, and then making a note of those settings for current and future use. I can recall a time at a race meeting where it was noticed that the carburettor was leaking fuel and the car had to be on the starting grid in 12-15 minutes. That carburettor was removed and put to one side, the spare carburettor was got out of its box and set to the settings as written down in my 'settings book.' That's float levels checked, jets changed, idle mixture adjustment screws set, throttle arm adjustments made, accelerator pumps set, etc. It was all done within 10 minutes and the engine was fired up and it ran perfectly. There was no thinking or dithering about what the settings should be, every adjustment was quickly made based on the collected and collated data accrued through previous testing. I knew exactly what basic settings were required, and we could look at the failed carburettor later to find out what was wrong with it. It can't be stressed enough that everything on an engine has to be narrowed down to the optimum setting, and an accurate record kept of each and every setting for future use. Race day is not the time to 'think' about settings as there's never any time to do this.

If the starter motor can't turn over the engine easily, each and every time, with anything more than 14 degrees of static ignition timing (that's the starter motor being able to turn the engine over and start it with 15 degrees some of the time with 16 degrees being too much ignition timing most of the time or anytime), 14 degrees of ignition timing is the sensible maximum able to be used. If your engine idles best with 16-18 degrees of ignition timing and the spring tension of the mechanical advance mechanism has not allowed the ignition timing to start advancing at the particular idle speed, you'll just have to accept the fact that the engine is going to idle with 2 degrees less than optimum because the starter motor has to be able to turn over the engine and it start it on every occasion. The advance mechanism springs are there to cause the total amount of ignition timing to be 'all in' or present at a particular rpm for maximum efficiency (the production of maximum torque, for example) so they're set for that requirement. It's a fact that you can't achieve all of the optimum parameters in all instances easily. In this example the idle speed ignition timing can't easily be set at the optimum, but it's pretty close, and isn't really going to be the cause of any initial off-idle acceleration problems. You run into this sort of problem when the total ignition timing can't be 'all in' until up in the rpm range, meaning quite firm mechanical advance mechanism springs have to be used. It's sometimes possible to use two advance springs where only one of them is installed in the distributor under tension and the other becomes under tension when the distributor is turning 250-500rpm/500-1000 engine rpm. There are all sorts of combinations possible here but it will take time to arrive at the optimum one.

An engine can likely be set with 14 degrees of static ignition timing, and have 16-18 degrees of optimum ignition timing for idling purposes, when the total ignition timing can be advanced at such a rate so as not to cause 'pinking' at low rpm, such as 2500-2750rpm. It's when the ignition timing can only be 'all in' at something like 3750-4000rpm, when quite strong advance mechanism springs have to be used, that having a low static ignition timing and a higher idle speed ignition timing might not be possible (or easy to achieve) with a combination of advance mechanism springs.

It's sometimes easier, as a result, to settle for the highest amount of static ignition timing that allows the starter motor to reliably start the engine, and the advance mechanism spring tension to cause total ignition timing to be 'all in' at precisely the right part of the rpm range, and not worry too much about the fact that the idle speed ignition timing might not be quite optimum. This does mean that your engine might actually be running with 14 degrees of ignition timing when, in fact, it really needs 16-18 degrees, but it's an acceptable compromise if it avoids starting problems. Unreliable starting is a nuisance that you can do without!

At some point in the testing stage the engine will likely become over-advanced, and a degree of roughness will become evident. At no stage should the amount of idle advance be set above 20 degrees. What you're looking for is the amount of degrees (within the range of 8-20) that provides for maximum smoothness and the highest rpm possible. This optimum setting should be used provided the engine will start without kickback.

With the idle speed ignition timing more or less settled, try 'leaning' the idle mixture off a bit to see if the smoothness improves. When the engine starts to slow and misfire slightly, go the other way and richen the mixture. When you have gone too far the idle will start to sound 'heavy' and the idle speed will start to slow. The midway point between the two is the optimum.

If the starter motor won't consistently turn over the engine at the optimum idle ignition timing setting, the timing will have to be retarded until it does. This is a compromise, but there's nothing that can be done about it except change the advance mechanism springs to allow a different ignition timing advancing regime, or fit a more powerful starter motor. Most starter motors are quite strong these days and, frequently, high torque starters are available within a range of engines, especially the large capacity versions of the same range.

The tone of the exhaust is also a useful guide in determining the optimum idle advance setting, though the fuel mixture does play a part in this too. Go to the end of the exhaust pipe/pipes and listen to the engine. The lightest sounding exhaust pipe means the best fuel burning with the particular engine concerned. A heavy sound means insufficient advance and, possibly, too rich an idle mixture. Excessive advance and the engine will have a perceptible but light miss; this, too, can be partially attributed to too lean an idle mixture. If a particular ignition timing amount within the possible range sounds best (exhaust note), advance the ignition timing 2 degrees from this amount and, if the engine still sounds good but not quite as good, retard the ignition timing by about 4 degrees to see what the effect is. Usually, the rpm will reduce and the engine's idle will get a bit rougher (slightly). Advance the ignition timing back to where it was before and try to 'pick' the point of maximum smoothness.

Do this a few times to get the 'feel of it.' The maximum amount of ignition timing to use is always pinpointed by the fact that the rpm does not increase (from the recommended idle speed) once a certain number of ignition timing degrees is passed. It then becomes a case of what number of ignition timing degrees less is the position to chose. There is usually a 2 degree 'window' on most engines which can be regarded as the optimum ignition timing. This means that if an engine idles well with 12, 13 and 14 degrees of ignition timing, you can try to narrow down which position of the three is best. With high octane fuel you would go to the high side because the engine won't 'pink' anyway. With an engine which has a high compression and the octane rating is a bit close to not being enough, you would go to the low side. That's the sort of thing it gets down to, to make you chose a particular ignition timing setting.

The optimum idle ignition timing setting coupled with the correct mixture (lean side) will result in an engine that idles without any intermittent, light misfiring, and there will be a minimum of exhaust pulsing at the end of the exhaust pipe/pipes (place the palm of your hand within 6 inches/150mm of the end of the exhaust pipe to check this). In some instances it's possible to have no pulsing at all and just feel the heat of the gases on your hand.

Exhaust lambda and % CO levels will also be low when the ignition timing is correct (have been narrowed down). It isn't unusual to have a standard engine or a racing engine registering idle mixture readings of 0.09-0.92 lambda/3.3-2.6%

Conversion chart		
Lambda	Air/fuel	%CO
0.80	11.8	8.0
0.81	11.9	7.3
0.82	12.0	6.5
0.83	12.2	5.9
0.84	12.4	5.4
0.85	12.5	5.0
0.86	12.6	4.85
0.87	12.8	4.35
0.88	13.0	3.8
0.90	13.2	3.3
0.91	13.4	2.85
0.92	13.5	2.6
0.93	13.7	2.15
0.94	13.8	1.9
0.95	14.0	1.6
0.96	14.1	1.4
0.97	14.3	1.0
0.98	14.4	0.8
0.99	14.6	0.6
1.00	14.7	0.5
1.01	14.8	0.4
1.02	15.0	0.3
1.03	15.1	0.15
1.04	15.2	
1.05	15.4	

CO irrespective of the idle rpm, or even less in some instances, such as down to 0.93 lambda/2.1% CO. You most definitely will not get an engine to idle at these sorts of figures unless the ignition timing has been narrowed down to within 1 degree of the optimum setting. It's a combination of the two that is required.

The conversion chart will prove to be useful if it becomes necessary to compare readings from different diagnosis equipment.

Chapter 12
Establishing ideal total ignition timing

The shape of the combustion chamber dictates to a large degree the total amount of ignition advance that an engine is going to require to give complete combustion. Efficient combustion chambers require less total ignition timing to produce maximum torque than combustion chambers that are less efficient. By choosing a setting related to combustion chamber shape (see chapter 3) the full advance setting will be right or very nearly right (within 1 or 2 degrees, for example). Using a setting established via combustion chamber shape, and then road/track/dyno testing the combination to prove beyond all doubt that the ignition timing full advance setting is the optimum one is the best option.

These days, data on the amount of total ignition timing that the various popular engines require is much more widespread, what with the massive amount of information and information swapping that goes on over the internet. Thoroughly testing an engine to find the optimum amount of ignition timing isn't quite as necessary as it was in days gone by. For example, in many instances today engine builders just set what they know to be the proven amount of ignition timing into an engine and, when the engine is first fired up it doesn't really need to be altered. For example, everyone who works on small block Ford V8 engines knows that one of these engines fitted with Ford Racing GT-40 'Turbo Swirl' aluminium cylinder heads will need about 36 degrees of total ignition timing. What should happen is that the engine should be checked on a rolling road with a plus and minus range of settings, and a decision made as to whether 34, 35, 36, 37 or 38 degrees is best for the particular engine based on power readings. From that point on the engine will always be set at the optimum figure. Before the first practice on race day, for example, the position of the distributor will ALWAYS be checked to make sure that the known correct figure is being realised in the engine.

Not all engines fall into this category, of course, and some have to be fully tested to ascertain their ignition timing requirements.

You don't have to know what the combustion chamber shape is to determine or find the optimum amount of ignition timing that produces maximum torque, though it can be very helpful to know roughly what the amount of ignition timing is going to be. Essentially, if you don't know what the optimum amount of total advance is for the type of engine you're using, you will have to test the combination to find out exactly what the amount of total ignition advance is going to be. With some knowledge of the likely amount, the distributor can to a certain degree be pre-built (not have too much mechanical advance in the distributor, for example).

The ideal amount of total ignition timing is that which causes an engine to develop maximum torque. An engine develops maximum torque at the point of maximum charge density (maximum amount of air in the cylinder). After this point has been reached, the maximum charge density (volumetric efficiency) slowly starts to reduce as the rpm rises. The reduction in charge density is quite slow, which is why most engines have a reasonably wide band of torque. At the point of maximum charge density, the amount of ignition timing has to be just right. Too much ignition timing and the engine will 'pink' and not develop the optimum torque, too little and the engine will not develop the maximum foot pounds of torque it is capable of. It's a critical aspect to achieving optimum engine power and it has to be tested for. After the point of maximum torque has been reached and the charge density is starting to reduce, the prospect of 'pinking' also reduces. After the point of maximum torque has been reached the amount of ignition timing is less critical, meaning that it can stay the same as the engine rpm increases or be increased slightly as the rpm increases above the maximum torque rpm. An engine will not 'pink' as the rpm rises past the point of maximum torque if the ignition timing remains the same because there is less air in the cylinder (less volumetric efficiency).

Some engines respond to a reduction in total ignition timing from that required to reduce maximum torque at or near maximum power, while some respond to an increase in ignition timing. The increase is easy to accommodate with the careful use of advance springs in the mechanical advance mechanism, but a reduction in a mechanical distributor is not. This is one of the advantages of a programmable engine management system, the engine can be checked for optimum ignition timing throughout the rpm range and the optimum amount of ignition timing built into the system. You can't really beat this. What you can do with a distributor-equipped engine is check

to see if the engine responds to an increase in ignition timing at high rpm (the top $1/3$ of the rpm range). Most don't, but it is worth checking just in case. Unfortunately, quite a few distributor-equipped engines respond to a reduction in ignition timing (2-4 degrees at most).

Finding maximum torque is easy on an engine dyno or a rolling road/chassis dyno as, with the engine on wide open throttle and under load, there is an amount of rpm where the maximum amount of foot pounds possible will be registering. The ignition timing is altered (increased and reduced) at this point, and the mean amount of ignition timing found by test. The details are noted for future use.

In days gone by, when racing engines were dyno tested the ignition timing was set at maximum torque, but the actual number of degrees wasn't actually measured, or it didn't have to be measured. Engines were set by test (set where maximum torque was produced) as opposed to setting them to degree markings on the flywheel or crankshaft against a pointer. After every rebuild the engine was dyno tested and the ignition timing simply reset again. There was no need to know what the actual number of degrees were. This was all very well for engines that were being used and maintained in this sort of environment, but it wasn't so good if you bought such an engine and then rebuilt it elsewhere. The optimum ignition timing setting needed to be known so that the engine could be reset to that amount. Even today a huge number of people do not realise the absolute importance of ignition timing in making an engine perform to its maximum potential.

The ideal test method involves the direct testing of the engine using full throttle from just after the camshaft has 'smoothed out' and before the point of maximum torque, through to 500rpm before maximum rpm using one gear,

and preferably top gear, over a measured distance against the clock. The distance must be set to suit the particular car and engine combination: it's no use having the engine reach maximum rpm, it must still be accelerating and pulling strongly at the end of the test distance.

The one thing an engine which doesn't have enough total ignition timing will not do is accelerate as quickly as one with the optimum amount of total ignition timing, so the time taken to cover the distance is very important. Once the full amount of ignition timing advance has been reached there is no more to be added and the engine will only be able to use the advance built into the distributor and this factor can be used to advantage in determining optimum total advance.

The least amount of spark advance required to achieve the maximum rpm as seen on the tachometer/rev-counter in the quickest time over a set distance is the correct amount of safe ignition timing advance. This assumes that the engine has the right air/fuel mixture ratio and does not have too much compression for the octane rating of the fuel being used.

Reminder! If your engine has too much compression for the RON and MON octane rating of the fuel being used, the test procedure is still totally valid, but the numbers will almost certainly be less than the generally known ones for the particular engine. If your engine is 'pinking' under wide open throttle from the point of maximum torque and above in the rpm range, it has too much ignition timing (provided the air/fuel mixture is correct and not lean). Engines with a sensible amount of compression for the octane rating of the fuel being used allow the optimum amount of ignition timing to be built into the engine.

For track testing proceed as follows. With the total advance set at the estimated figure (set with a strobe light using the crankshaft damper/pulley total advance mark with no vacuum advance connected) the vehicle is tested by checking the acceleration in top gear, or the next gear down, over a measured distance and up to near maximum rpm and the time taken to cover the distance. A straight is ideal, but not absolutely necessary.

Two stakes will be required, one to set the start of the measured distance and one to set the finish. The stakes are positioned trackside at suitable distances to allow the car to accelerate in top gear or the next gear down from a set rpm each time. The first stake is approached at an appropriate amount of rpm and, as the car is level with the stake, the accelerator pedal is fully depressed as the stopwatch is set going. The engine accelerates and, when the second stake is reached, the stopwatch is stopped. The second stake must be far enough from the first to allow the engine to reach 500rpm before the point of maximum power or the second stake must be reached before the power surge has finished. To do this correctly the engine will have to be tuned just right. Each engine will vary in its requirements according to the degree of modification but the test procedure is identical for all.

On the rolling road, the engine can be tested in a similar manner, acceleration wise, power reading wise, by starting off in first gear and going through the gearbox through to maximum rpm in top gear. If the engine is going to misfire for any reason it will do it now, although the true rate of acceleration is difficult to assimilate, but the amount of total ignition timing required to produce maximum torque/ maximum power will be correct as found on the rolling road dyno (within 1 degree). The air/fuel mixture can be monitored while this is being done and richness or leanness can be spotted. A good rolling road operator can get an engine extremely close and very 'race

ready' mixture wise, but what you can't do in this environment is allow for the atmospherics (air density). The track testing method is superior because the engine is working in the actual operational environment, and where the air density can be monitored and the engine set exactly to the individual day-to-day air/fuel mixture requirements. Rolling road dyno the engine first, then track test, and then race it.

SUMMARY

If you're still not sure what amount of total ignition advance your engine responds best to, test the engine again using 26, 27, 28, 29, 30, 31, 32, 33, 34, 35, 36, 37, 38, 39 and 40 degrees of total ignition advance (unless your engine has a hemispherical combustion chamber, in which case start the testing at 34 degrees, then try 35, 36, 37, 38, 39, 40, 41, 42, 43 and 44 degrees of total ignition advance). One, two, or perhaps three of these total ignition advance settings will result in a better overall rate of acceleration. Always use the lowest figure which gives the fastest rate of acceleration. One thing is for sure: while some of the settings might take time to arrive at, there's no doubting whatsoever that once you have all of the settings right, your engine will respond instantly, from off idle to maximum rpm. It's very satisfying to drive a car with an engine that isn't 'fussy' because the ignition timing regime is correct.

If your engine is over-compressed for the RON and MON octane rating of the fuel being used, one or two of the above settings is still going to cause the engine to go better, even if it's 'technically' too retarded, or the ignition timing has had to be retarded to stop the 'pinking' under wide open throttle acceleration. You can't allow an engine to 'pink' violently under wide open throttle acceleration because, besides it not being a good thing mechanically for

any engine, the rate of acceleration will not be optimum. Keep retarding the total ignition timing until the 'pinking' stops. If, when the 'pinking' is stopped, the engine performance just isn't satisfactory, there's really only one option left and that is to reduce the compression ratio and start again.

If your engine has a non-standard production camshaft fitted to it, and most cars enthusiasts cars tend to do this, you do have to be able to pick the point in the engine's power curve where the camshaft 'smooths out' and starts to 'make power.' This point is often a bit difficult to find at times, as it usually happens over a 100-200rpm range. You find it by slowly increasing the engine rpm from idle in 100rpm increments and suddenly the rpm of the engine will increase by several 100rpm without further movement of the accelerator pedal. The point can be narrowed down to within 100rpm by carrying out this procedure a few times. When you acceleration test your engine in top gear, the starting rpm for the test must be 100rpm above this point.

Some engines are fitted with camshafts which have far too much duration for the application. They might sound good at idle, etc., but they are next to useless when it comes to giving solid results. Many factory-made high-performance camshafts are much better than people give them credit for, yet for the most part they are discarded as quickly as possible. For most applications, there's no point in having a camshaft fitted to an engine that starts to produce power at 4500rpm when the mechanical strength of the engine limits the maximum rpm to 6000 or 7000rpm and/or the cylinder head design means that the point of maximum power is at about 7000rpm. Camshafts like this exist, and plenty of people buy them with high expectations. What most people really want is a camshaft that starts producing power as low down in the rpm range as possible, and the point of maximum efficiency of the camshaft to be as closely matched to the point of maximum cylinder head efficiency as possible. This factor is missed by about 90% of people who buy aftermarket camshafts.

All engines have a point of maximum power on the basis of cylinder head efficiency as opposed to camshaft efficiency. This point is often lower than most people would like to think it is. You can get quite good at picking the rpm point of maximum power (to within 100rpm). For example, as a general rule, most two valve per cylinder pushrod-operated engines (hemispherical combustion camber type engines excluded) produce maximum power at about 7000rpm. If you take the most highly developed two valve per cylinder engines of this type, such as a 'Ford Racing' small block V8 engine, which was specifically developed by Ford USA for racing purposes, the point of maximum power is still only going to be in the vicinity of 7400-7500rpm; and these engines are the best of the best of the type. This means that pushrod two valve per cylinder engines, as well as many of the single overhead camshaft ones with similar type combustion chambers, need to be tested up to but not exceeding 6500-6800rpm to ensure that the point of maximum power is not exceeded during acceleration testing.

Finding the optimum amount of total ignition timing for any engine is quite vital, and it isn't all that difficult to do in the final analysis. It really just involves careful testing, and using a lot of slightly different settings to narrow down the final and optimum setting.

FUEL OCTANE RATINGS

There is a great deal of confusion surrounding petrol/gasoline octane ratings, with very few people having any understanding of the matter at all. The vast majority of fuels commercially available around the developed world are unleaded, but many countries still don't have emission controls on engines using unleaded fuel, and many are still using tetraethyl leaded fuels. The leaded and unleaded issue aside, as this has nothing to do with the octane aspect of fuels, there are two basic tests used worldwide to determine the octane ratings of petrol/gasoline used in cars. The two test methods are the Research Octane Number (RON) and the Motor Octane Number (MON).

In the late 1920s, a fuel sample testing method was devised for determining the octane ratings of petrol/gasoline mixes by the Co-operative Fuels Research Council (CFR) in the USA. This resulted in the development of a very special single cylinder engine, which had variable compression ratio and ignition timing. This engine is commonly referred to as a CFR engine. The very same engine is used to test fuel samples for RON and MON using two different testing regimes or methods. Before a fuel sample is tested, the CFR engine is calibrated using a pure chemical mix 'reference fuel' which, because of its specific chemical content, is guaranteed to be 100 octane.

A sample of fuel to be tested for octane is used to run the engine. The RON method of obtaining an octane rating sees the CFR engine run at 600rpm with a set amount of ignition timing as prescribed by ASTM D2699/IP237 (13 degrees Before Top Dead Centre). This rating is regarded as being representative of the particular fuel which will cause an engine to go at start up and idle. ASTM stands for American Society for Testing and Materials, and D2699 is the criteria of its RON test. IP stands for Institute of Petroleum and 237 is its number for this test regime (same test).

The same sample of fuel is again used to run the engine and the MON method of obtaining an octane rating is conducted under ASTM D2700/IP236 criteria. The CFR engine is run at 900rpm, the compression ratio is increased and the ignition timing is advanced. The octane rating derived from this test is regarded as being representative of how the particular fuel sample will cause an engine to go on the road at cruise conditions or motorway driving. You virtually never see a MON rating displayed on a pump in a service station, but the two ratings are used by all petrol companies around the world. BS4040, for example, lists a minimum requirement for both RON and MON but you only ever see the RON rating displayed on a pump.

The UK still has leaded fuel available. When tetraethyl lead fuel was generally phased out in 2000, the British Government allowed 1% of the total amount of petrol made and sold in the UK to be leaded. The petrol companies that decided to make this fuel and appoint selected outlets to sell it, used 0.099gm per litre of tetraethyl lead, which provides acceptable valve seat recession protection for road use but it's not good enough for racing use in an engine designed to have fuel that offers protection going though it. This fuel is 98 RON and 86.2 MON. This fuel will eventually be phased out.

Two unleaded fuels have been available in the UK for some time now: Premium unleaded, which is required under BS7070 to have a minimum RON of 95; and Super unleaded, which is required to have a minimum RON of 97. There is a slight problem with Super unleaded if the petrol station holding it in its tanks is not a busy one. Super unleaded gets its extra octane by having various 'volatiles' mixed in it, and these evaporate quite quickly. The longer the fuel remains in the tanks of the petrol station, the lower the octane rating of the fuel. Premium unleaded does not have these volatiles in it and, as a result, maintains its manufactured octane (95) rating longer. In some instances, Premium unleaded will cause your car to go better than Super unleaded, which may seem odd but this is the reason for it. As with all petrol/gasoline, if maintaining the octane is important (if you're using a high compression engine, for example) the fresher the fuel the better, and the recommendation is to buy your fuel from a busy forecourt. In certain circumstances, old Super unleaded fuel can end up with a lower octane rating than Premium 95.

The highest RON octane unleaded fuel readily available in the UK, for example, is BP Ultimate 102 (102 RON/90 MON) Tesco 99 Super Unleaded (99 RON/87 MON) followed by Shell V-Power (98.1 RON/87.5MON) with these fuels being made the BS EN 228 (2004) which requires a minimum/maximum 101-102 RON and 89-90 MON. These three fuels with TetraBOOST mixed in with them are approximately equivalent to the old Five Star high octane leaded fuel of many years ago (quite knock resistant). Note that petrol companies do make competition use only versions of these fuels made to BS EN 228, and they are absolutely guaranteed to be 102 RON/ 90MON. Formula One uses this sort of fuel. In the UK, and for use in reasonably high compression engine racing purposes (11.0:1 through to 12.0:1) you can't really do better than to use BP Ultimate 102 with TetraBOOST mixed in with it on the basis of cost versus availability for use in an engine which doesn't have (or can't have) hardened valves seats fitted into it. It's a changing situation and the RON and MON ratings of new fuels as they are introduced need to be checked against existing ones. The higher the better in both cases, especially the MON rating.

The USA, while still using the RON and MON tests to rate fuel, has gone another way by introducing an anti-knock index number (AKI), which is based on the RON and the MON added together and then divided by 2. Other names for this system you see used in the USA are PP (Pump Posted) or perhaps PON (Pump Octane Number). As you can see, when you're talking octanes, you need to be quite clear what criteria are under discussion.

There are three basic grades of AKI street legal unleaded fuels on sale at the pumps, with slight variations in the Premium unleaded fuels plus a very low octane Regular unleaded (New Mexico 85 AKI octane). For the purposes of matching the fuel available to a compression ratio that will be suitable, use the RON ratings of the US fuels listed. Take it that, on average, Regular unleaded 87 octane is suitable for use with 8.3-8.8:1 compression engines, Mid-grade unleaded 89 octane is suitable for use with 8.8-9.2:1 compression engines, and Premium unleaded 91 AKI octane is suitable for use with 9.0-9.3:1 compression engines. Add 0.3 for 92 AKI octane and 0.7 for 93 AKI octane. Altitude comes into the picture here as, at high-altitude, the air is less dense and the octane rating can be lower. There is quite a difference from sea level to 5000 feet for example.

Regular unleaded 87 octane is 91 RON – 83 MON
Mid-grade unleaded 89 octane is 94 RON – 84 MON
Premium unleaded 91 octane is 96 RON – 86 MON
or 92 octane is 97 RON – 87 MON
or 93 octane is 98 RON – 88 MON

For high octane street legal unleaded fuels, and for 'off road' racing purposes, USA enthusiasts are fortunate compared to those in other countries, because there is a vast array of specially mixed and blended fuels available. You can find out more about the following companies' product by checking their websites:

VP – http://www.vpracingfuels.com
Sunoco – http://www.sunoco.com
F&L Racing Fuels – http://www.fandl.com
Sports Racing Gasoline – http://www.cosbyoil.com

If you look at Sunoco's GT100 street legal unleaded fuel, for example, which is advertised as being 100 octane, this fuel has a rating of 105 RON and a 95 MON, making it pretty good fuel for road use. The 100 octane rating you see advertised is the AKI. This fuel will run a naturally-aspirated A-series engine with up to a 12.5:1 compression ratio without any problem. Sunoco also makes an unleaded fuel called GT Plus, which has a rating of 109 RON and 99 MON, and will run a racing engine with a 14:1 compression without problems. VP C10 Performance Unleaded is an equivalent fuel to Sunoco GT100 and the street legal VP Motorsport 103 is equivalent Sunoco GT Plus. A lead substitute additive will have to be used with these latter fuels in conjunction with 'soft' A-series cylinder heads to prevent valve seat recession.

For racing purposes, Sunoco makes 'Standard Leaded,' which has a rating of 115 RON and 105 MON, and contains 0.99gm of tetraethyl lead per litre. 'Supreme Leaded' has a rating of 114 RON and 110 MON, and contains 1.12gm of tetraethyl lead per litre. Finally, 'Maximal Leaded' has a rating of 118 RON and 115 MON, and contains 1.32gm of tetraethyl lead per litre. VP and Sports Racing Gasoline make equivalents. These sorts of leaded fuels will run any A-series racing engine extremely well. All of these specialist racing fuels are simply excellent, but they are quite expensive.

Avgas used to be readily available for automotive racing use around the world. This fuel was often repackaged by the major fuel companies in 20 litre cans and sold as racing fuel. There was a time when the price was virtually the same as the highest octane fuel available at the pumps. New Zealand, for example, still has petrol stations which sell 'Race Gas' from a normal fuel dispensing pump, along with the 91-97 RON unleaded fuel normally available. The Challenge petrol station on Manukau Road near Pukekohe racing circuit sells this fuel out of a pump for the convenience of racers for racing purposes only (illegal for road use). This 'RaceGas'/Avgas is 107 RON and 100 MON, making it pretty good stuff; and, with approximately 0.8gm per litre of tetraethyl lead in it, you don't burn valve seats out. The price is higher than regular 97 RON octane unleaded fuel, but it's not that much more expensive.

Avgas used to be known as 100/130, the 100 part referring to the MON rating while the 130 was the supercharge octane rating test number applicable for the times when military and commercial aircraft engines were largely all super-charged. The RON number wasn't all that applicable. How the world has switched from leaded fuel to unleaded fuel is quite interesting.

In the mid-1960s, the California Air Resource Board (CARB) decreed that all new cars sold in the state (starting 1966) would be required to have emissions controls fitted to them, in an attempt to clean up the air in the LA basin (smog being a big problem at the time). Starting in 1968, the US Federal Government decreed that all cars sold nationwide were to have emissions controls fitted to them. In 1970, Congress passed the 'Clean Air Act' and established the Environmental Protection Agency (EPA). Also in 1970, 'low lead' content fuel, which had 0.5 grams of tetraethyl lead in it per US gallon was introduced, and 1971 model USA cars were built with low compression ratios to run on it. Up until this time fuel could have up to a maximum of 4.0 grams of tetraethyl lead in it per US gallon for the highest octane fuels available, even though 2.5 grams per US gallon was typical. Existing engines had been modified to meet these new requirements and, while emissions levels reduced by about 50%, the miles per gallon nearly halved and many engines started failing with valve seat recession problems (not quite enough lead in the fuel to prevent it!). The measured lead content in the air however did start to reduce. Catalytic converters were being fitted to all USA cars from 1975. For 1977, all USA made car engines had to be able to run on unleaded fuel; the cylinder heads had either hardened exhaust valve seats fitted into them or the exhaust valve seats were induction hardened. The rest of the developed world has slowly followed suit as the years have gone by.

Auto industry engineers repeatedly told USA Federal Government officials that the way to go would involve much development and would take time. Their idea was to develop all new engines that could run on unleaded fuel. The petrol companies would develop high octane unleaded fuels so that high compression ratios could be used which would see a minimum of fuel used on an over-all basis. The general idea was maximum efficiency by squeezing every last bit of energy out of every gallon of petrol/gasoline. In the meantime they suggested that the levels of lead in fuel could be drastically reduced but not down to 0.5 grams per gallon, more like 1.0 gram per US gallon initially. This would have been a reduction from 2.5-4.0 grams to 1.0 grams, and there would have been few failures. They were largely ignored by those in power who knew little about what was involved, and it's taken 30 years and many trillions of gallons of extra fuel burnt inefficiently to get to where we are today. The skies of LA are finally beginning to be clear most of the time and it could be due, in part, to the use of modern engines like the excellent modular Ford V8, for example, with its high compression ratio, efficient burning design cylinder heads, high octane unleaded fuel requirement, Lambda 1.0 focused engine management system and minimum fuel usage technology.

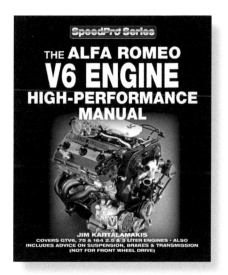
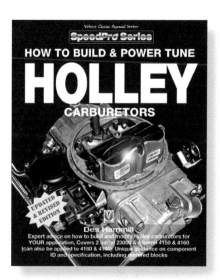

Index